Lean Into Grace

Let God's Grace Heal Your Heart, Refresh Your Soul, and Set You Free

ESTD 2016

YELLOW POPLAR

PRESS

By

Stacey Pardoe

Praise for *Lean Into Grace*

Grace, wisdom, and understanding are infused throughout the pages of this book. Stacey is a born storyteller who offers an open-hearted vulnerability in the gentle way she illustrates her words with personal vignettes. Her beautiful writing draws the reader into learning God's truth about what it means to be His beloved children who lean into His grace instead of self-effort.

Dawn Klinge, author, Historic Hotels Collection

For women trying to sustain their marriages, nurture their children, and serve God by the sheer force of their will, *Lean Into Grace* will land like "good news from a far country!" Stacey Pardoe shares her own discovery that the grace of God would indeed hold up under the weight of her brokenness, that it was sufficient to overcome shame, and to sustain her through the mind-numbing routine of daily mothering. What a relief to be reminded that Jesus comes alongside the believer with sinewy love—a love not dependent on our accomplishments, willpower, or flawless faith pedigree.

Michele Morin, Bible teacher, speaker, and blogger at Living Our Days

GRACE. It's one of my favorite words in the entire dictionary! And, my friend Stacey Pardoe has written an entire book about grace...grace to ourselves, others, and grace from God. Whether you need grace in your hurts, failures, sin, relationships, or in how you treat yourself, this book addresses all of this and more. I highly recommend this new book and suggest every woman get her own copy!

Melanie Redd, author of *Just Rest: A 90-Day Devotional Journal*

Every time I pick up one of Stacey's books, I feel like I'm sitting down with a dear friend to talk about the beautiful ways God is able to help us and give us everything we need. She has this wonderful ability to apply faith to everyday events in a humble and transparent way that always blesses me. I highly recommend that you *Lean Into Grace* with Stacey and learn about the ways God is able to heal your heart and refresh your soul.

Deb Wolf, author, and writer at CountingMyBlessings.com

Stacey is a friend I trust to speak the truth over deep and vulnerable places in my heart. *Lean Into Grace* is no exception. If you have wondered how to live this Christian life, this inspiring book is for you. It is a tender and beautiful invitation to surrender our self-efforts and learn how to receive God's grace. Heart-warming and hope-giving, *Lean Into Grace* is a must-read for all who struggle to experience God's victory, freedom, and healing in their lives.

Hadassah Treu, award-winning Christian author, blogger, poet, co-author of over 10 devotional books, and writer at onthewaybg.com

To every person who is tired of feeling stuck in destructive habits, worried thoughts, and overwhelming emotions, God is inviting you to lean into his grace, and he will do the work of setting you free.

Contents

Introduction

A million stars glance down from the inky canopy overhead, and I stand at the window feeling empty inside. Today was a long day spent racing to meet writing deadlines, running errands, and keeping up with the kids.

I know what I should do to fill the emptiness. I should go somewhere quiet and spend time with God, read a book, or snuggle up with the little ones. Instead, I succumb to temptation and begin searching the cupboards for something chocolate. After coming up empty in the kitchen, I head to the laundry room where my eye catches the box of candy on the top shelf. I buy this candy with the intention of using it for Easter egg hunts and sharing it with the kids on special occasions. Sadly, it has also become my secret source of escape and comfort.

Opening the box, I remove the foil wrapper from a peanut butter-filled Easter bunny and devour it. The bunny is delicious, and I indulge in another. And then another. One at a time, I unwrap the chocolate bunnies and shove them into my mouth like an addict.

On one level, I feel numb, and feeling numb feels good. On another level, I feel disgusting. I hate that I keep failing when it comes to establishing a healthy relationship with food. I fear I'll never find freedom from this addictive cycle. I've been relying on willpower to help me change my unhealthy eating habits for decades. Sadly, willpower consistently fails me. I wonder if I'll be stuck forever.

Redefining Grace

Like me, perhaps you've been relying on self-effort and willpower for transformation in some area of your life. Maybe you're trying to stop yelling at your kids, heal your marriage, or cultivate a thriving relationship with God. Perhaps you've been trying to lose weight for as long as you can remember, and you're frustrated by your repeated failures to stick with any of the diet plans you've tried. Despite your best efforts, nothing seems to work. You feel stuck. Every failure feels like one more piece of evidence that you'll never step into the freedom and victory you long for.

Maybe you've heard that God's grace is all you need, but you're not sure how God's grace could transform the secret sins, unhealthy habits, and behavior patterns you can't seem to change.

In his book, *Renovated*, Dr. Jim Wilder redefines grace as, "God acting in our lives to accomplish what we cannot accomplish by our own abilities."[1]

The first time I read these words, Dr. Wilder's definition of grace spoke to the part of me that was tired of failing and wondering why willpower rarely produces lasting change in my life. I realized that God was inviting me to lean into grace, letting *him* accomplish what I had been unable to accomplish in my own strength. God was waiting to heal my relationship with food, help me overcome my greatest insecurities, infuse my relationships with joy, and set me free from every stuck place in my life.

Your Invitation to Lean Into Grace

Our culture has taught us that the secret to success is mustering more willpower and self-effort. Let's be clear: There's nothing wrong with trying hard. Colossians 3:23 tells us to put our whole hearts into everything we do. However, we need to make a distinction. Pouring our whole hearts into God's assignments—and leaving the outcomes in his hands—is very different from relying on self-effort alone to bring the change we want to see in our lives.

This book is my story of learning to lay down self-effort, lean into God's grace, and create more space for him to work in my life. Additionally, these pages are your invitation to stop striving in self-effort and let God do what you've been unable to do for yourself. We will create space to let God set us free from fear, worry, stress, shame, besetting sins, and more.

Before we begin our journey together, return with me to the laundry room where I'm stuffing my face with expired Easter candy.

God's Grace Is Sufficient

Within just a few short minutes, I've lost track of how many chocolate bunnies I've eaten. Too many. I feel like the Apostle Paul, who wrote, "For the good that I want, I do not do, but I practice the very evil that I do not want" (Romans 7:19).

The last thing I want to do at this moment is turn toward Jesus. I'm not even sure I want to stop eating this chocolate. However, in an act of desperation, I pray these words: "Jesus, I'm stuck. I need you to work in my life and do something I cannot do for myself. I need you to heal my relationship with food and set me free from this awful cycle."

Nothing particularly startling happens. Instead, a familiar truth comes to mind: "My grace is sufficient for you, for my power is perfected in weakness" (2 Corinthians 12:9).

As I consider the words, I sense God inviting me to exchange self-effort for surrender. I recognize that no matter how hard I try to honor God, I'll still make mistakes. However, God isn't asking me to be perfect; instead, he wants me to experience his chain-breaking power as he works in my weakness.

As I hold the box of chocolate on my lap, part of me wants to eat one more bunny. Nevertheless, compelled by a force I cannot explain, I shove the candy back inside the box, put the box on the shelf, and return to the living room to join my family.

In some ways, tonight was another failure in my relationship with food. In another way—a deeper way—it was one small step toward the freedom I crave. I'll tell you more about this journey later in our time together.

God is inviting you to lean into his grace, allowing him to set you free as well. Let's take our first small step into grace together.

Notes:

1. Wilder, J., & Willard, D. (2020). *Renovated : God, Dallas Willard & the church that transforms*. Navpress.

1

Grace for Your Hurting Heart:
Crying in the Bathroom

Grace Takeaway: We lean into grace when we turn to Jesus in our brokenness instead of trying to run from our pain or fix what feels broken in our lives.

Morning light pierces the smudged windowpane like a golden ray of hope. After a string of grey days, the dancing sunbeams encourage my weary heart. Climbing from warm sheets, I feel hopeful—like maybe this long season won't last forever.

I'm eight weeks pregnant, and the weeks have been passing at a slow crawl. I'm trying not to worry, but this pregnancy has been weird. After debilitating sickness throughout my first two pregnancies, I've barely felt nauseated this time. I'm trying not to be nervous about what the lack of sickness might mean. Maybe it's a gift from God.

After breakfast is served and our daughter heads off to school, I turn on a cartoon for our three-year-old and head into the powder room to freshen up. Alone in the tiny room with the plum-colored walls, I have no way of knowing that my life is about to be turned upside down. In the amethyst glow of the bathroom, I discover what no pregnant woman wants to see. I'm bleeding.

My mind races through every concern from the past weeks: not feeling sick, my sunken abdomen, no cravings for chicken nuggets for breakfast, and waking up with energy instead of nauseated exhaustion. It hits me like a gut punch, and I immediately know I'm miscarrying.

"Oh no," I whisper as a dozen different emotions flood me in an overwhelming stream of disbelief, disappointment, sadness, and fear.

Sitting with my head in my hands on the closed toilet seat, I feel the urge to look toward heaven and ask the most obvious questions: *Why is this happening? Why couldn't this all work out like we hoped—as we planned? Why now? Why me?*

I imagine you've had this moment, too. The circumstance you feared became your reality. The worst-case scenario swooped in and became the crisis on your doorstep, and you put your head in your hands and asked why. Your heart broke into a thousand tiny pieces, and the grief threatened to suffocate you.

I attempt to swim through the deep waters of my scattered emotions and get my bearings as I sit in the bathroom. My knee-jerk response is to find my phone and text my three closest friends before hurrying to call my mom, my husband, and the doctor. I'm about to leave the room in a state of panic when something stops me. I sense a soft and quiet invitation. It's an invitation to take a deep breath and draw close to my heavenly Father *first* in this moment of devastation.

I will call the doctor. But I will press close to Jesus for a few minutes first.

It seems preposterous, but before I pick up the phone, I slip into the quiet of the basement to connect with the One who holds my days in his hands.

As I sit in the silence, I consider the medical truth regarding my situation: Many women experience bleeding throughout pregnancy and deliver healthy full-term babies. This is possible in my case, but my intuition tells me otherwise. I've had a hunch this might happen for weeks.

In the stillness, I let my mind sort through my wide array of emotions. On some level, I am afraid. I'm afraid of what the days ahead will hold. I'm afraid of what my body will have to endure as we walk through the nitty-gritty part of this loss.

I'm also heart-broken. I had dreams and hopes for this child. I was looking forward to another August baby. I was imagining stroller walks on cool autumn days and rocking our little one beside an open window on warm September nights. My dreams have been dashed.

The Death of Hope

We all face times of pain, sorrow, and brokenness. In these times, we lose more than our dreams. It often feels as if hope has died with our dreams.

When these times come, self-effort often goads us to hurry through the valley of sorrow and escape the pain. Meanwhile, the gentle voice of God's grace says, *Bring your brokenness to Jesus and let him do what you cannot do for yourself—let him shape your heart to look more like his heart in this valley of sorrow.*

I invite you to walk with me through the heart-wrenching journey of our miscarriage as we have an honest conversation about letting God's grace carry us through times of heartache and loss. We'll begin by talking about the many ways we deal with pain and sorrow in our human strength. Then, we'll explore what it might look like to walk through heartbreak with Jesus, and I'll share four ways to stay close to Jesus during painful times.

I pray the Lord will show you what it might look like to let him breathe hope and healing into your broken places as well. Return with me to the basement, and we'll talk about the ways we cope with sorrow and sadness.

Relying on Human Strength When Hope Is Lost

As I sit in the quiet of our basement and try to make sense of what is happening, all I can think about is how I might fix this sad situation. The voice of self-effort tells me I can heal our broken hearts by making sure I get pregnant again before the daffodils emerge in the springtime sunlight. Nobody has to be sad. I can totally fix this!

I'm just about to find a calendar and begin hashing out my plan when the voice of grace offers a vastly different invitation. The voice of grace whispers, *Don't put your hope in fixing this situation with another pregnancy. Put your hope in the fact that Jesus is with you right now, in the middle of this tragedy.*

Most of us are experts at fixing what is broken. When sickness strikes, we have dozens of medications ready for this precise moment (or we're quick to rush to the drugstore for a remedy). We carry bandages, blankets, gloves, hats, flashlights, sewing kits, and loads of snacks in our cars. We like to be prepared, and we thrive on the sense that we are always ready to save the day.

It's not wrong to fix what's broken in our lives; however, when we put our hope in fixing broken situations, we circumvent healing encounters with Jesus, our Living Hope. Meanwhile, Jesus invites each of us to lean into grace by putting our hope in his presence with us—not in our abilities to restore what feels broken in our lives.

Have you been trying to fix an area of your life that feels fractured? Maybe you've been trying to control a loved one's addiction, heal a hurting friend's broken heart, help your child get back on track, or cheer up a family member who has been discouraged for far too long. You've been orchestrating detailed plans and putting your plans into action.

Let's be clear: there is a time to take action. There is a time to get out of bed, come up with a plan, and take steps to move beyond our pain. However, there's a big difference between putting our hope in our plans and putting our hope in Jesus' presence with us.

It's important to note that not everyone responds to crisis situations by immediately shifting into "fix-it" mode. We might respond by analyzing, withdrawing, or ignoring difficult circumstances. Some of us cope by filling ourselves with food, distracting ourselves with entertainment, or fulfilling ourselves through workaholism.

Regardless of how we cope with sadness, every time we turn to sources other than Jesus for hope and healing, we plant our feet on unstable foundations. We leave little room for Jesus to heal our hearts and transform us into his image through our pain.

Walking Through Heartbreak with Jesus

When our hearts are hurting, it's tempting to sprint through the valley of grief. More than anything, we want the sorrow to pass, and we want to feel "normal" again. We often avoid our difficult emotions because they're painful, and we want to escape the pain and discomfort.

As we attempt to avoid our pain, the Lord offers a different invitation: Instead of hurrying through our difficult emotions, Jesus wants us to walk through our heartbreak with the ongoing awareness that he is at our side.

Like a good Shepherd leading his sheep through a dark valley, Jesus promises to stay close during our broken seasons. He is Immanuel—*God with us*—and he will never leave us.

Throughout the past decade, I've discovered several practices that have helped me draw near to the Lord in times of heartache. Return with me to the snowy day of the miscarriage, and I'll share examples of each of these practices.

Worship

After my moment in the quiet of the basement, an afternoon at the hospital confirms the sad news. We lost the baby. My husband comforts me as we process our loss together, and at the end of the long day, I crash into bed feeling entirely emotionally exhausted.

Early the next morning, I descend the stairs, sink into the soft cushions of the couch, and put a worship playlist on the computer. I'm staring at the wall and feeling numb when the words of a song draw my attention to the screen. The words worshipfully speak of God's goodness, and it seems they were written just for me with my torn-in-two heart.

Immediately, I know I have a choice: I can turn off the computer and brew coffee, or I can worship God in the middle of my pain.

I don't feel the presence of Jesus with me. I feel empty and alone. Part of me feels the urge to turn away from God, pretend this isn't happening, and try to embrace a "normal" day. Meanwhile, a deeper part of me knows that doing the hard work of grieving in God's presence is the secret to healing, and I make the difficult choice to stay on the couch. I lift both arms in worship, close my eyes, and begin to softly sing along with the words of the song. Lifting my arms in the living room feels a bit awkward, but I do it as a sign of my surrender.

I have not cried over our loss yet, but I weep as I worshipfully declare God's goodness amid my heartbreaking loss. It is the purest moment of worship I have ever experienced.

As I sob, I sense the tender love of the One I worship. I know he is moved by my worship. I know this is the pivotal moment in which I have not hardened my heart or taken offense in my pain.

Friend, this is the place where healing begins. If you can sit with Jesus in the middle of your sadness and lift your heart in worship, he will begin a deep work of healing within you. It might not *feel* like God is good. Praise him anyway. Praise him because his goodness is not contingent upon our feelings.

When we worship God in our pain, we give him open access to begin healing our hearts. Grieving in the presence of God offers consolation we will find nowhere else. Yielded praise awakens a broken soul to the very real presence of the One who will never abandon us. As we awaken to his presence, his presence begins the work of healing our hearts.

Do you know what else happens when we worship with broken hearts? The enemy is defeated with his own weapon. Satan would like nothing more than for you to harden your heart and turn away from Jesus when you feel wounded by life. Trust me. I've lived this out. Tragedy and heartbreak are the enemy's weapons, and he means to destroy you with them. He will succeed if his weapons lead you to turn away from God. However, when the enemy's attacks lead you to run to Jesus and worship him with your broken heart, the enemy loses. Christ is exalted, and in the process of exalting him, we are strengthened.

Lamentation

In addition to worshiping God, it's important to create space to release our emotions in his presence. For me, this often happens during worship.

As I worshiped God the morning after the miscarriage, I also poured my heart out to him. I told him everything I was feeling and asked hard questions. I held nothing back and wasn't afraid to approach him with my overwhelming emotions.

Our emotions often feel consuming during times of loss. It's not uncommon to feel sad, angry, regretful, hopeless, and fearful at the same time. Lamentation is an expression of mourning that helps us release our emotions. It might include sobbing, yelling, wailing, and even physical expressions like punching a pillow. We tell God everything we are feeling and let it all out.

Releasing our emotions in the Lord's presence through lamentation is a healthy way to avoid burying our anger, sadness, or other difficult emotions. Buried emotions easily lead to bitterness and offense toward the Lord. When this happens, Satan gains a foothold in our hearts, and our healing is hindered.

Lamentation helps us keep soft hearts. Instead of burying our negative emotions, we release them, and this release prevents bitter roots from growing within our hearts.

God's Word

After pouring our hearts out to the Lord in lament, it's important to plant our feet on the truth of God's Word. God uses Scripture to renew our minds and change the way we see our circumstances. A friend often reminds me that instead of ignoring or running from our emotions, "feelings are meant to be felt." However, after we process our emotions through lamentation, it's important to return to God's truth.

Staying engaged with God's Word helps us move toward healing, recognize the difference between our feelings and God's truth, identify the fiery darts of the enemy, and find an anchor to steady us in life's storms.

As our family mourned the loss of our little one, the Lord led me to stand on the promise found in Hebrews 6:19, which reminds us that God's hope is a reliable and ever-present anchor for our souls.

These words reminded me that my hope is found in Jesus' presence with me—even in the middle of tragedy. Every time I felt tempted to put my hope in getting to the other side of our grief or getting pregnant again, I returned to the anchor of my soul: the hope of Jesus' ever-present love.

If you are hurting and don't know where to turn in your Bible, reading one Psalm per day is a good place to begin. The Psalms are filled with emotional outcries from hurting hearts and are a great place to turn when our hearts are broken.

Fellowship with Others

In addition to worshiping, lamenting, and planting our feet on God's Word, spending time with others is an important part of walking through grief with Jesus. Most of us feel tempted to isolate ourselves in times of grief and loss. However, Jesus designed us to live in community with others. We heal in community. We need friends and loved ones to help carry our burdens, provide safe spaces for us, and pray for us. We need counselors, pastors, mentors, friends, and seasoned believers to speak into our pain.

As for me, I felt tempted to isolate myself after our loss. I didn't feel like explaining our difficult situation or answering questions about the sorrow written on my face. Nonetheless, I knew I needed loved ones to help carry me through my grief. When my husband asked how I was doing, I told the truth. I let him hold me on the couch as we worked through our emotions together.

When my mom called me on the phone, I answered. Every evening, I took a walk down our country road and talked to her on the phone. Sometimes, we talked about how I was doing. Most of the time, we talked about other things, and simply being present with her was deeply healing for me.

My closest friends arrived at our house with meals, gifts, and invitations to get together. These precious women reminded me that I wasn't as alone as I often felt.

I close with a gentle reminder for you today, precious friend. In times of loss and sadness, prioritize your closest relationships. Let your mom, your sister, or your best friend minister to you. Resist the urge to isolate yourself. Jesus often uses other people to bring hope and healing to our hurting hearts.

Questions for Reflection and Discussion:

1. What part of your heart does the Lord want to heal? Have you given him access to the pain, or are you holding back? What is stopping you from opening your heart to him?

2. In what way do you typically respond to loss and sadness? Do you try to fix it, run through it, analyze it, or ignore it? How does this typically work out for you?

3. Describe a situation in which you felt tempted to put your hope in your ability to fix your unpleasant circumstances. What is the difference between circumstantial hope and hope in Immanuel—*God with us*?

4. Have you ever had the experience of lifting your heart in worship during a tragedy in life? How did this kind of worship change you?

5. Conclude by finding a Bible verse to stand on in times of sadness. Spend some time in worship before the throne of God. Let him minister to your heart as he desires—as only he can.

2

Grace for Fearful Circumstances:

Turning the Enemy's Weapon against Him

Grace Takeaway: We lean into grace when fear becomes a prompt that sends us running to Jesus' arms instead of a force that consumes, paralyzes, and breaks us.

Eleven Months After the Miscarriage

It's a frigid January morning, and heavy frost encases the pale, grey earth. Last year's miscarriage feels like a dim memory, and I'm five months pregnant with what appears to be a healthy baby. Unlike the pregnancy with the baby we lost, I've been couch-bound with severe illness for months. The diagnosis is called hyperemesis gravidarum. For me, it looks like nine solid months of throwing up, headaches, dizziness, and symptoms that outshine the worst imaginable case of the flu. I spend my days staring at the ceiling, feeling like I've been poisoned, and longing for the day when this child emerges from my body and the illness finally lifts.

Today, I'll need to leave the couch for a follow-up appointment in which my doctor will review the results of last week's 20-week ultrasound. I've been so consumed with the illness that it hasn't occurred to me that anything could be wrong with our baby. My primary focus for this day is on not vomiting in public.

I arrive at the office ten minutes early, and after the nurse ushers me into the white-walled exam room, the doctor enters with a nervous expression on her face.

"Your little one's arms and legs look good. The growth is right on track, so that's good," she says. The tone of her voice tells me she's setting me up for bad news. I try to dismiss it and focus on not throwing up on her.

"We did notice a defect in the baby's heart," she says—her eyes shifting uneasily.

Immediately, the room becomes blurry, and I hear only the thrumming of my panicked heart hammering in my ears. I notice the doctor is still talking. She's using acronyms I don't understand, and even if I did understand, I wouldn't hear a word of it through the cloud of fear that's now surrounding me.

I'm not sure how long I sit in the haze, but it finally dawns on me to start asking questions. I ask a dozen off-the-cuff questions about things she probably already explained when I was in the fog three minutes earlier: *Will it require surgery? Will our child die? What do I do next?*

She has very few answers. She refers me to a pediatric cardiologist, kindly asks if I have any more questions, and leaves me sitting in a paralyzing haze of fear. My baby has a heart defect, and I feel helpless, alone, and terrified.

Consumed By Fear

Few circumstances elicit more fear in a mama's heart than a threat to the life of her child. In the weeks after discovering our unborn child's heart defect, fear became my constant companion. Mustering my willpower, I was determined to fight. I was determined to will my way toward victory over fear. My fear-fighting strategy included repeating Bible verses, filling our home with worship music, rebuking the devil, and praying like crazy. Everything would be all right. It *had to be* all right.

Four weeks into the fight, I realized willpower was failing me. I was tired of tossing and turning all night with dreams about open-heart surgeries and fears for the life of our child. I remember thinking, *There has to be a better way to navigate this.* Sadly, I had no clue what that better way might look like.

Sweet friend, I hope you can't relate. I hope you've never stared into the future with weak knees and tried to navigate beneath an incapacitating cloud of fear. But I also know life is hard. Jesus promised trouble in life, and when trouble comes, fear often follows. Today, you might be facing fear about a diagnosis, a troubled child, a distant friend, an ailing loved one, an unstable job, a dwindling bank account, or any one of a thousand different fear-laced circumstances.

You might cope with fear by white-knuckling your way through life's difficulties until the circumstances shift. Maybe you fight fear with prayer and Scripture, and you secretly feel like a failure when you can't seem to shake the fear. You wonder if God is disappointed with your lack of trust, and the fear mingles with the shame you feel about your flimsy faith. *Ask me how I know.*

When Your Faith Feels Flimsy

After several weeks of silently grappling with fear for the life of our child, I asked a close friend to come to my house and sit with me as I lay nauseated on the couch. She held my feet on her lap as the winter sunshine pierced the windowpane, and I told her everything about our baby's heart defect and my awful battle with fear.

"I feel like such a failure," I confessed. "If I just had stronger faith, this fear wouldn't be controlling me like it is. I want to enjoy the miracle of this child growing within me—not spend every moment freaking out about the future."

My friend tenderly put her hand on my knee and said something I'll never forget.

"What if you stopped being controlled by fear and turned the enemy's weapon of fear against him?"

"What do you mean?" I asked.

"What if, every time you felt the fear, you used it as a prompt to remind you to run to Jesus' arms?" she suggested.

The voice of self-effort had been telling me that it was up to me to overcome my fear. My friend's advice was vastly different: Grace doesn't ask us to defeat our fears in our strength; instead, grace invites us to run to Jesus in our fearful moments—and *Jesus* will do the work of pushing out the fear.

When trials come, most of us sincerely want to stand on the promises we memorized under sunny skies. However, when troubles leave us reeling, it's not easy to stand on the assurances we memorized when life was going well. Fear creeps in, and it often feels insurmountable.

Even amid our greatest fears, there's good news for us all: God isn't asking us to muster up more faith and defeat our fears on our own. Instead, he invites us to run into his arms and let *him* push out the fear for us.

How do we run into Jesus' arms and let him push out our fears?

Today, I'll share several ways Jesus led me to run into his arms as we waited to meet our unborn child: He invited me to relinquish my worst-case scenario; he led me to a Spirit-breathed Bible verse to speak when I felt fearful; and he taught me to use worship as warfare.

These practices weren't about trying harder. They weren't ways of pushing out the fear in my strength; instead, they were pathways into the arms of the One who was capable of pushing out the fear for me. Today, we'll look at how these three principles might help you lean into God's grace when it comes to your fears as well.

Relinquishing Your Worst-Case Scenario

As I wrestled with how to run to Jesus' arms in my fearful moments, I reached out to a mentor asking for advice. My wise friend responded with words that went something like this: "What's your worst-case scenario? When you can trust Jesus with your worst-case scenario, fear will begin to lose its grip."

I wrestled with her words for a few days. Dozens of awful scenarios filled my mind.

Finally, on a warm winter morning, I realized I was most afraid of losing our baby. It hurt so much that I didn't even want to consider it. Meanwhile, my mentor's words streamed through my mind: "When you can trust Jesus with your worst-case scenario, fear will begin to lose its grip."

"I'm not sure I can trust you with this, Jesus," I whispered.

In the silence, the following thought came to mind: *All the days ordained for this child's life are already written.* I recognized them as the words Psalm 139:16.

It was as if Jesus was reminding me that I wasn't in control of the outcome of our child's future. Our baby belonged to Jesus, and even if our baby's ordained days didn't match my hopes and expectations, those days were already written. Jesus was asking me to trust his divine plan.

As I sat in the morning light, I held my trembling hands over my rapidly expanding belly—the very place where our little one's heart thrummed with its beautiful rhythm. "Jesus, I give you this worst-case scenario. Even if the worst thing happens—even if this little one does not survive—I trust that you are still good. I trust that you will carry us through even the most horrible scenario. I surrender this child's life into your hands. Trusting you with this feels hard to me. Lord, help me to trust you more," I whispered.

Slowly, a noticeable shift took place in my spirit. Peace covered me like a warm blanket. Jesus began the work of pushing out the cloud of fear that had paralyzed me for weeks.

As you look to the future, you might be facing some areas of uncertainty as well. I encourage you to dig beneath your fear and identify your hypothetical worst-case scenario. As specifically as possible, name this scenario. If the worst outcome were to take place, what would that look like?

After naming your worst-case scenario, ask Jesus to help you trust him even if this situation becomes your reality. This is a work you cannot do without the Holy Spirit. You cannot trust God without the movement of the Spirit in your life—and this movement is always a work of grace. It might take some wrestling to come to the place where trust in God pushes out your fear of the future. Keep wrestling. Keep asking God for grace to trust him more. This prayer is his will for you, and he fulfills our requests when we pray according to his will (1 John 5:14).

Speaking God's Word

After relinquishing your worst-case scenario, planting your feet on the firm foundation of God's Word will help you push back against fear.

Most of us know we're supposed to claim Scripture and stand on God's promises when life unravels. Interacting with God's Word is always a powerful discipline; however, there's a difference between fearfully muttering Bible verses and wielding Spirit-inspired truths as declarations over our lives and the lives of our loved ones.

When fear ravages our hearts, we need more than a list of verses to recite each morning. We need the Holy Spirit to breathe life into God's Word. We need to stand on God's Word with our full weight—believing that what he says is true and that it directly applies to our lives.

Before my friend encouraged me to use fear as a prompt to send me running to Jesus, I was regularly declaring all sorts of Bible verses about fear. I had good intentions, but I was losing the battle. Fear had paralyzed me and stolen my joy. I was losing the battle because I needed God to do a work of grace within me: I needed him to carry his Word from my head to my heart. I needed a Spirit-breathed Word to empower me and uphold me. There's a big difference between speaking God's Word with a half-believing heart and speaking his Word like we're wielding fiery swords.

The moment Psa m 139:16 came to mind, something different happened. It was as if God spoke directly to me and said, "All the days ordained for this child's life are already written. You can trust me." A spark was ignited in my spirit, and the words were more than a promise I knew in my mind. They made it to my heart and came to life. By God's grace, I knew the words to be true for my baby's life, and the truth pushed out the fear.

Every time I spoke the verse, I declared—to myself and to the spirits in the heavenly realms—that our child's days were already numbered. My role was to steward the assignment of carrying our little one within my body as I cared for us both. The outcomes were never mine to control or carry.

Speaking God's Word is a sure way to run to Jesus' arms when we face fear, but I encourage you to go deeper than making a list of fear-fighting verses. Ask God to do something within you that you cannot do for yourself. Ask him to show you a specific verse that speaks directly to your fear and ask him to carry the truth of the verse from your head to your heart. Through the power of the Holy Spirit, ask him to help that verse sink into the very marrow of your bones.

Every time you feel fear arise within you, speak the verse God imprinted on your heart. Take your eyes off the fear and fix them on Jesus instead. This is how we run to Jesus in our fears.

Using Worship as Warfare

Lastly, I invite you to join me as I traveled to the pediatric cardiologist seven weeks after discovering the defect in our unborn baby's heart. God's grace had been helping me rise above fear, but the stress of the day had me feeling unnerved. After waiting to see the doctor for nearly an hour, I waddled into the dimly lit room and lay on the thin paper that covered the cold examination table. For a quick moment, fear paralyzed me. I realized the trajectory of our future would be greatly influenced by the outcome of the ultrasound.

With my heart racing in my chest, I asked God to push back the fear for me. Without delay, the lyrics of a song I'd been singing for a few weeks ran through my mind. I'd been listening to "Raise a Hallelujah" by Bethel Music, and as the song played in my mind, it led me straight to Jesus' arms. My focus shifted from fear to the power and authority of our great God. Much to my surprise, peace fell upon me as the doctor examined our little one. I was reminded—without a doubt—that God held the life of our baby in his hands. I also knew he would carry us through any diagnosis.

Twenty minutes later, I walked out of the office with the results of the examination in my hand. The heart defect had not healed in the past seven weeks. In one sense, our future was uncertain. However, in a different sense—a truer sense—I had never had more peace about the future. Worship flowed from my heart as I declared my trust in the One who promised to go with us into the unknown.

Like a Spirit-breathed Bible verse, a worship song that touches your heart with Jesus' love can be a powerful weapon in your war against fear. Ask God to lead you to a fight song that will help you run to Jesus, and he will use that song to push back the fear. To this day, when I hear the song "Raise a Hallelujah," something stirs deep within me. I imagine Jesus fighting the forces of darkness and defending our precious baby.

The Battle for Your Mind

In the weeks following my appointment with the pediatric cardiologist, I came to a surprising realization. All along, I thought we were in a battle for our child's healing. There was certainly a battle taking place in the physical realm; however, the primary battle wasn't about a heart defect. The primary battle was a fight between fear and trust, and the battle was won the moment fear lost its grip on me.

Precious friend, the trial you are facing extends far beyond a medical condition, a financial crisis, a struggling loved one, or an uncertain situation. There might be a battle taking place in the physical circumstances surrounding you, but the physical realm is not the most important part of the battle.

The battle for your mind holds far more weight than any physical battle you might be facing. It's a battle to choose fear or faith, worry or trust, discouragement or hope. Choose to be ruled by fear, worry, or discouragement, and you give the enemy a foothold in your life. However, when fear prompts you to run to the arms of Jesus, Jesus will defeat the enemy with the precise weapon intended to take you down.

Satan wants fear to consume your mind, prompt you to make rash decisions, and lead you away from God. He wants to use fear to paralyze and distract you. He wants fear to rule over you—to become the object of your worship.

Instead, when fear becomes a prompt that leads you to worship Jesus, Satan is defeated with his own weapon. Just as worshiping God in times of heartbreak heals us (as we discussed in Chapter One), worshiping amid fear leads to victory over fear. Friend, worship is warfare.

Questions for Reflection and Discussion:

1. Did a specific fear regarding future circumstances come to mind as you read this chapter? What did God reveal to you about this fear?

2. Find a quiet place and walk through the relinquishment process described in this chapter. Surrender your worst-case

scenario to God and ask him to help you believe in his goodness, even if the worst-case scenario becomes reality. Share any reflections from your experience.

3. Ask God to show you a biblical truth to replace your fear. Write it in your journal or in the space below. Try to memorize it. Hang it where you'll see it. Hide God's Word in your heart to help you when you face fear in the future.

4. Jesus stands victorious over the enemy right now, and by aligning yourself with him, you are victorious too. By trusting him with your worst-case scenario, standing on God's Word, and lifting your heart in worship, you stepped into the victory Jesus already won for you at the cross. Journal any response to this victory and thank God for his power in your life.

3

Grace for Your Fear of Failure:

Embracing the Part of You That Can Never Change

Grace Takeaway: We lean into grace when we let God's love push out the fear of failure.

I gaze out the window as the dawn awakens over chartreuse fields of goldenrod. Birdsong cascades through the poplar, and I inhale slowly. I hold my breath for a moment before breathing out. As I focus on breathing, my diaphragm expands, my soul settles, and my mind quiets.

I begin most days at this window. This is where I meet with the Lord. It's where I give thanks, press into my Father's love, and create space to assess the rhythms of my day.

Today, I'm celebrating the new season our family is settling into. Aiden James was born on a foggy Wednesday morning two weeks ago, and our family pediatrician has seen no signs of a defect in his little heart. We'll visit the pediatric cardiologist in a couple of weeks for a closer look.

For now, our focus is on learning to navigate life with three children. Everyone in our family is adjusting to this radical shift in our family dynamics.

Eight-year-old Bekah transitioned home for summer break the day after Aiden entered our lives, and four-year-old Caleb is adjusting to no longer having full reign of the house.

I'm so thrilled to be free from the sickness that kept me couch-bound for nine months that I'm making up for lost time. Completely ignoring the fact that I'm recovering from my third C-section, I hustle from one task to the next feeling like a rockstar as I clean out the fridge, catch up on laundry, and finally wipe the sticky handprints off the walls.

My dear husband aims to be helpful while staying out of the way of his miraculously revitalized wife.

Life has turned upside down for us all.

When Life Feels Overwhelming

As I sit by the window and reflect on our new season, I feel immensely grateful. I'm thankful to be healthy after nine months of pregnancy sickness, grateful for three beautiful children, and overwhelmed with joy as little Aiden seems to be flourishing.

After relishing these gifts for a few moments, I shift into my daily discipline of reviewing the previous day to examine my words, attitudes, and actions.

"Father, what do you want to show me about the past day? Search my heart and show me what you want me to know," I pray.

As I sit in the silence, a scene from the previous day replays in my mind. I spent the entire morning hustling from one task to the next: cleaning the house, nursing Aiden every 90 minutes, and tending to the various needs of the older two children. Instead of stopping to eat lunch, I decided to undertake my least favorite role as an ambitious mom: haircuts. I'd been putting it off, and Caleb's hair was getting shaggier with each day.

I called him into the kitchen, wrapped him in a sheet, and wasted no time getting to work.

As I trimmed his bangs and gazed into his sapphire-blue eyes, I paused to admire him. I noticed the freckles on his cheeks and the way he wrinkled his nose as he smiled. For an instant, I was pulled out of the undercurrent of stress that had threatened to carry me away all morning, and I was fully present with my boy. I wasn't hurrying or striving or focused on producing anything.

"Lord, help me live present to these fleeting moments—thankful instead of stressed," I whispered as I moved to the top of his head and kept clipping.

The prayer had barely left my lips when Bekah called from the living room, "Mom! I think Aiden pooped! It's leaking onto the floor."

Bekah was keeping an eye on baby Aiden while I played barber. Bless her heart. She's just not into changing diapers quite yet.

I was instantly drawn out of my grateful reverie and plunged back into the reality of my life. I made the split-second decision that poop trumps a haircut, commanded Caleb not to move, and raced to the living room with a jug of carpet cleaner.

Much to my dismay, by the time the poop was removed from both the floor and the better half of Aiden's body, his big brother had fled the scene of the haircut. A trail of brunette clippings enabled me to trace his footprints, and I discovered him eating a lollipop in his bedroom closet. As I questioned where the lollipop came from, the sound of water boiling over on the stovetop reminded me that I was also cooking a full stockpot of vegetables.

I wish I could say that I took it all in stride, waved a playful hand, and laughed. Instead, I unfurled in anger. I screamed for Caleb to get back to his chair, angrily commanded Bekah to find the vacuum and sweep up Caleb's trail of hair (as if any of it were her fault), and let baby Aiden fend for himself in the playpen (he was screaming, of course) while I tended to the mess on the stovetop.

An hour later, the stovetop was clean; Caleb's hair looked presentable; and most of the scattered hair clippings had been gathered. I attempted to redeem the day by taking the kids for a swim in the creek, but I spent most of the time barking orders as they complained about the smoldering summer heat and swarms of biting black flies.

Not my best day.

As I sit by the window at the dawn of this new day, I reach an unsettling conclusion: Throughout the past two weeks, I have been hurried, stressed, and overwhelmed almost constantly. On one level, I'm grateful for this season of life with young children. On a different level, I feel like I can't keep up, and I fear I'm failing.

My house is never as clean as I'd like it to be. Dinner is rarely prepared by the time my husband arrives home from work. Caleb doesn't know his alphabet yet, and Bekah hasn't even opened her summer reading workbook. The laundry baskets are never empty, and I live with the looming sense that I'm falling behind.

I feel out of control, and this feeling leads me to snap impatiently at my family, hurting the ones I love most.

As I reflect on these difficult truths in the morning light, I recognize that I don't want to be the flustered mom everybody tries to keep pacified. I don't want my kids to choose their words only after checking my expression and assessing my ever-changing moods.

Instead, I want to be kind-hearted and full of grace. I want to be the kind of woman who laughs often and easily. I want to live with deep joy in my heart and exude a kind of love that makes people feel safe with me.

Sadly, when I'm rushing from one task to the next in my quest to avoid "falling behind," I am not living like a light-hearted, grace-filled woman.

"Show me what you want me to know about the pace of my life and the state of my soul, Lord," I pray.

A gentle impression washes over me, and I realize that I've fallen back into the trap of finding my identity through what I can produce and achieve. Sadly, this isn't the first time I've fallen into the pattern of finding my identity through my performance.

As a teacher, I often felt crushed when my students failed. On one level, I knew that their grades and behaviors weren't mine to control; however, I often had a deep sense that if I had performed better as their teacher, they would have succeeded.

As a young wife, I felt defeated when my husband offered suggestions about how I might be more supportive or expressive. When I felt like I was making him happy, I felt great about myself. When I saw my flaws, I shriveled in shame and felt like my failure defined me.

Now, as a full-time mother and keeper of our home, I feel accomplished and peaceful when the house is clean, the kids are thriving, and I sense that I'm serving my husband well. However, I feel like a failure when the house is a wreck, the kids are unruly, and it's been months since the last date with my husband.

Because I fear failing as a mom and wife, I listen to the voice that tells me to hustle, check off every box, produce, achieve, and prove my worth through what I'm able to accomplish. Self-effort leads me to fill my schedule to overflowing, make sure I crush the entire to-do list every day, and push harder—regardless of the cost.

Dear friend, I wonder if you can relate. Perhaps you feel exhausted by the pace of your life and the demands of your days. Beneath this full schedule—beneath these high expectations you've set for yourself—maybe you're a bit like me. Perhaps you've started to find your identity through your performance.

When you perform well, you feel secure, confident, and joyful. However, when you fall short, you feel like a failure, and you are shaken to the core.

I wish we were taking a slow walk down a country road together instead of meeting within these pages. I wish I could stop our walk, look into your eyes with all the compassion in my heart, and tell you that I get it.

You see, throughout the past two decades, God has been incrementally teaching me to find my identity in his love instead of finding my identity through my performance. Obviously, I have not arrived. Nonetheless, by his grace, the Lord is slowly transforming me. He uses moments like my morning moment by the window to gently redirect me after I slip back into the fear-based performance mentality. In these moments, he guides me onto solid ground by reminding me of my identity. I've learned that when I am secure in my unchanging identity, I have nothing to prove. I am no longer ruled by the fear of failure.

Let's spend the remainder of this chapter learning how to overcome the fear of failure by embracing our true identities.

The Part of You That Can Never Change

The most effective way I can explain the truth about the unchanging part of your identity is by inviting you on a journey with me. This truth is so foundational that we need to unpack it carefully, and I pray that my story can help you claim this same truth for yourself.

My journey began shortly after my 29th birthday when my husband and I discovered that we were expecting our first child.

We were thrilled. We'd been dreaming of becoming parents for four years, and the reality of our news felt almost too good to be true.

Two weeks after discovering our life-changing news, I met my friend Kathy for coffee after work on a sunny spring afternoon. After just one sip of coffee, my stomach turned. A dizzying cloud of nausea descended upon me, and I assumed I was coming down with a stomach bug. I apologized to Kathy for leaving early and headed home, where I spent the remainder of the evening hunched over the toilet. I had no way of knowing that I was about to endure months of debilitating illness.

A few days after the sickness began, I realized I was dealing with hormone-induced pregnancy sickness and not a virus. As I explained in Chapter Two, the sickness lasted until the end of the pregnancy. Because of the sickness, I was forced to take a medical leave of absence from my teaching job. I spent my days lying down while trying to stay hydrated.

In addition to the physical suffering, my emotions suffered as I was forced to step back from so many parts of my life—parts of life that were deeply embedded in my identity.

I was unable to teach my students or minister to the teens within our church's youth group. I had to step back from women's ministry, Bible studies, and writing. Throughout the worst months, I was too sick to even receive visits from friends, hold conversations with my husband, or read my Bible. Every label I had used to define myself was stripped away.

I couldn't make sense of the trial when I was in the middle of it; however, months after our beautiful baby girl came into the world, God showed me part of his purpose for my suffering. By stripping away almost every part of my identity, he showed me the only part of me that can never be taken away.

The only part of me that can never change is this: I am unconditionally loved by God. I am his beloved daughter. He fought for me, bled for me, and died for me. His love can never be taken away from me.

Friend, if you have received Jesus as your Savior, this truth applies to you as well. The only part of you that can never change is your belovedness in God's eyes. You are his precious child (John 1:12). He loves you so much that he demonstrated this love by sending his precious Son to die on the cross and receive the punishment you deserve (Romans 5:8). Your belovedness is the truest thing about you, and it is the only part of your identity that can never change (Romans 8:38-39).

Like me, you might find your identity by your job title, the roles you play within relationships, your hobbies, your leadership positions, or even your ability to read your Bible and practice traditional spiritual disciplines.

I hope you never have to endure a season in which these gifts are taken away. However, if you do, your heavenly Father wants you to know that one part of you can never be stripped away: You are his precious and beloved child.

Before we continue, it's important to pause and reflect on what it means to be a child of God. According to John 1:12, everyone who receives Jesus as Lord and Savior becomes a child of God. Those who have not received Jesus' gift of salvation are not yet God's children.

A wise, older friend once reminded me that every human being on earth is on a journey with Jesus. Regardless of where we fall on the road with Jesus, we are all somewhere on the road. You might be decades into your journey of walking with Jesus, or perhaps you have not yet received his sacrifice and asked him to be your Savior.

Today, I challenge you to consider your journey with Jesus. If you have received Jesus as Lord and Savior of your life, then the promises in this chapter—and throughout this book—are for you. However, if you have not yet decided to follow Jesus and receive him as Savior, I invite you to pause right now—or whenever you are ready—and turn to page 273 to learn more about how to become his follower. When you decide to follow Jesus and receive his gift of salvation, every promise in the Bible is a promise directly for you.

From Your Head to Your Heart

I began following Jesus as a teenager, but it took decades for the truth about my identity to settle into my heart and transform my life. I intellectually knew Jesus loved me, but I couldn't comprehend what it might look like to live from the firm foundation of this identity.

Many followers of Christ haven't grasped the truth about their unchanging identities as Christ's beloved children because they feel unlovable. On an intellectual level, they know Jesus loves them. However, when they step back to look at their lives, they see a lot of messes. They see habitual sin patterns and areas in which they're sure they're disappointing God. They know God loves them, but they find it hard to believe he *enjoys* them.

I know all about this struggle because, for years, I was certain God was disappointed with me. Drawing near to him didn't feel like a life-giving invitation because I imagined he was mad at me. I imagined he was mad at me for not reading my Bible enough, losing my patience, eating my feelings, snapping at my husband, and falling asleep instead of praying.

During the years when I was wrestling with these thoughts, I discovered a passage of Scripture that radically transformed my understanding of God's unconditional love for me. God used the book of Hosea to forever change my perception of his love.

Hosea was a prophet during a time when God's people had turned away from him. They were participating in idol worship and had directly rebelled against God. God sent Hosea to warn the people that he was about to discipline them by sending trouble and hardship upon them. However, after warning them about this painful discipline, God offered the most surprising gift: a promise to allure his people in the same way a husband allures his bride. Hosea 2:14 reads, "Therefore, behold, I am going to persuade her, bring her into the wilderness, and speak kindly to her."

Some of us imagine God turning away from us in disgust when we wander away from him; however, this is not the image offered within Scripture. When we wander away from God, he looks for ways to draw us into his loving arms. The New Living

Translation of Hosea 2:14 reads, "But then I will win her back once again."

Like a husband who pursues and lovingly forgives the wife who betrayed him, when we turn away from God and intentionally pursue sin, God pursues us and looks for ways to draw us back into his love. Even while we are lost and wandering away from him, God considers how he can draw us into his love. This is a God who loves us without condition. This is a God who is deeply pleased to be with us.

Do you believe that God takes great delight in you and loves to spend time with you?

When we grasp God's joy in being with us, we will be changed from the inside out. Interestingly, discoveries in neuroscience show that God designed our brains to form secure attachments through joy-filled connections.[1]

Just as newborns attach to their caregivers through smiles and loving expressions shared in face-to-face interactions, all attachments are formed through joyful interactions. This includes our attachment to our heavenly Father. The secret to a stronger attachment to God is joyful interaction with him.

This joyful interaction might be as simple as spending five minutes each morning basking in the presence of God and reminding ourselves that he enjoys being with us. It might look like enjoying our hobbies while talking to God and listening to worship music.

During these times, we remind ourselves that God finds pleasure in being with us. We soak in the Lord's joy as we imagine him smiling upon us. He uses these moments to affirm our identities as his beloved daughters, and he fills our hearts with the confidence we find in his love alone.

What does all of this identity talk have to do with overcoming the fear of failure?

When we grasp our unchanging identities as God's beloved daughters, God's grace does a work we cannot do for ourselves. His love sets us free from the fear of failure because we no longer find our worth through our performance.

We know that God loves us no matter what. We can perform poorly or fail to perform at all, and we are assured that God still loves us. We are free to fail because we find our identities in God's love, not our achievements.

An Invitation to Let God Speak Into Your Identity

How do we position ourselves so that the truth about our unchanging identities moves from our minds to our hearts? I encourage you to spend a few minutes sitting with Jesus every morning. Find a quiet place in your home, imagine Jesus sitting with you, and bask in the truth that he loves you more than you can fathom. You captivate his heart with just one glance in his direction (Song of Solomon 4:9).

Close your eyes and imagine Jesus's expression as he enjoys spending time with you. Rest in his love and listen for his quiet whisper reminding you that he loves you.

Appendix A in the back of the book is a resource to help you meditate on God's truth about your identity as his beloved child. I encourage you to turn to the Appendix and soak in these truths for a few minutes every morning for the next 30 days. Research shows that it takes 21 days for a new thought to form in our minds. Spend the next month basking in the truth about your identity, reading these powerful statements out loud, and reminding yourself that you are God's child, and God will do a work in your heart. His Word will renew your mind as you begin to understand that failure can never define you. You are defined by your position as God's precious and dearly loved child.

Questions for Reflection and Discussion:

1. Do you ever feel crushed after performing poorly or failing in an area of your life that is important to you? What does this sense of failure show you about where you find your identity?

2. In what ways have you built your identity upon checking boxes off of lists or performing well? What is God showing you about finding your identity through your performance?

3. Do you feel like you are perpetually "falling behind" in any areas of your life? Have you considered that you might not be falling behind after all? What is God showing you?

4. Imagine God looking at you. What expression do you see on his face? Does this expression align with the truth that God is always happy to be with you?

5. In what ways would your life be different if you lived from the knowledge that your belovedness is the truest thing about you?

Notes:

1. Wilder, J., & Willard, D. (2020). *Renovated : God, Dallas Willard & the church that transforms*. Navpress.

4

Grace for Grumpiness:

Taking Yourself Less Seriously

Grace Takeaway: We lean into grace when we embrace humor and whimsy and learn to take ourselves—and our agendas—less seriously.

It's a balmy summer evening, and our family is finishing a relaxing dinner on the deck. I'm about to clear the table when Bekah winds up to throw her banana peel into our "compost pile" in the weeds. There's only one problem: I'm sitting directly between Bekah and the weeds.

I see it unfold in slow motion before the peel has left her hand, but my mouth is too full to intervene. Within seconds, an overripe banana peel smacks me hard in the face.

My immediate response is anger; however, I manage not to respond. Instead, time seems to slow down. I quickly scan the faces of my family members. They watch me with cautious expressions as they wait to see which direction the moment will take us.

Caleb stares slack-jawed.

Bekah stands frozen in the same position from which the banana peel left her hand.

My husband stares with an expression that's somewhere between smirking and ducking for cover.

As I scan their faces, I recognize that I am facing a pivotal decision. I can unleash in anger, or I can lighten up, see the humor in the situation, and laugh.

By the sheer grace of God, I take one deep breath, and then I choose laughter.

Instantly, I see the tension leave my family members' faces, and we all howl until tears roll down our cheeks. What could have been an angry moment becomes a funny memory we'll share forever.

Most likely, you've faced a banana-peel moment as well. You know how it feels to stand at a precipice and choose the way you're going to respond to a moment in which life just went off the rails. Your moment might have involved a disastrous mess in your living room, a loved one who did something ludicrous, a botched birthday dinner, a vehicle backed into a garage door, a dog who destroyed an entire room, a box of crayons discovered in the dryer one hour too late, or some other circumstance that threw you for a loop.

The moment your circumstance went awry, you faced a decision. You could choose to erupt in anger and frustration, or you could make the counter-intuitive choice to stop taking yourself so seriously, take a deep breath, and laugh.

I chose the better response in the banana-peel moment; however, far too often, I choose anger. Instead of laughing, I lash out and hurt the people I love most.

Sadly, just as a misplaced crayon can ruin a whole dryer filled with clothes, anger is destructive. Righteous anger can bear fruit, but anger born out of frustration disintegrates relationships.

Contrastingly, when we choose to lighten up and respond to frustrating situations with light-hearted laughter, we nurture relationships. Like cultivating a garden with tender care, we plant, water, and strengthen our relationships.

I want to be the kind of woman who knows how to laugh at myself. I want to learn to take myself—and my agenda—less seriously. I want to learn to be flexible with my plans and whimsical with my kids. Instead, I often hustle here and there with an aura of seriousness surrounding me. I act like I'm the most important person on the planet, and if I don't get the grass off the living room floor, the world just might stop spinning.

Have you ever met a woman who hustles around like she's on a life-saving mission everywhere she goes? Her face is always tense, and she doesn't have time to stop and chat because she has important things to do. This woman might be living "on mission for Jesus," but she makes it clear to the world that her mission is stressing her out. Instead of exuding warmth, gentleness, and love, she exudes a hard exterior and a grumpy, critical spirit.

How do I know about this woman? Sadly, far too often, I am this woman. I hate to admit it, but there were years when I thought my work for God's kingdom was so important that I huffed and puffed and made sure everyone knew how stressed and busy and important I was. Those years were the least joyful years of my life.

The closer I grow to Jesus, the more I sense his gentle invitation to slow down, cultivate joy in the work he calls me to do, and laugh freely instead of displaying my busyness and self-decreed importance. God has a sense of humor, but some of us are so busy trying to live "on mission" for God that we've forgotten how to laugh—especially at ourselves.

This lighter way of living generally doesn't come without a conscious effort to embrace it. The voice of self-effort tells us to be serious, stay poised, and make every minute count for something measurable.

Some of self-effort's suggestions are threaded with truth. There is a time to buckle down and be serious about the work God sets before us; however, there is also a time to lighten up and take ourselves less seriously.

Determining whether a situation calls for "on mission" focus or lightheartedness requires discernment, and I've learned that I usually have a deep sense of which kind of scenario I'm facing. A banana peel in the face is a moment to laugh about. Driving across town to meet with a friend who is facing a crisis is a serious moment, and it's not to be taken lightly.

Today, we're going to focus on learning to lighten up as we face life's banana-peel moments and daily inconveniences. In his grace, God invites us to respond to these moments by breathing deeply, loosening up, and laughing.

I invite you to join our family as we explore two circumstances in which God is inviting us to lean into grace and take ourselves less seriously. First, we'll talk about how to handle daily detours with grace. Second, we'll push out grumpiness as we create space for whimsy. Let's begin with a conversation about frustrating daily detours.

Leaning Into Grace When God Sends a Detour

A few days after the banana-peel incident, I promised the kids a trip to the public library. Bekah was determined to find the next book in the series she'd been reading, and Caleb had big ideas for a book about dragons. Little Aiden was less than thrilled to be strapped into his car seat on a hot summer afternoon, but he had no choice but to comply.

We arrived at the library to find an empty parking lot, and I immediately knew we'd picked the wrong activity for the afternoon. As we approached the entrance, the librarian passed us with the mail tucked under her arm. "Sorry, we're closed on Fridays," she said with a compassionate expression on her face.

Both older kids immediately burst into tears, and baby Aiden wasn't far behind them. After buckling everyone in the car for the second time in ten minutes, I said, "Well, where do you want to go today? We could go to the animal park. Or we could visit the spillway and check out the waterfall."

After a short discussion, we decided on a trip to the animal park, and we redeemed the day with ducks, lions, and a dancing mandril. When all was said and done, we were low on fresh reading material but energized by a fun afternoon with the animals.

Later in the day, as I reflected on our change of plans, I noticed a shift in my life. A few years ago, derailed plans generally sent me over the edge with stress. However, as God continues to smooth my rough edges, he has taught me a valuable lesson about leaning into grace: We live with grace when we hold our plans loosely—willing to receive God's detours with open hands.

I'm all about making plans. Sadly, my plans become idols when I hold onto them with clenched fists.

You might handle a change in schedule with grace and joy. But chances are, there's a certain situation that leads you to lose your cool. Imagine driving ten hours to a vacation rental, only to learn the scheduling company double-booked, and you suddenly have no place to stay for the week. Imagine a hurricane blowing into town on your wedding day or a virus sending your child to the hospital the day you were supposed to leave on an important trip for work.

It's not easy to hold our plans loosely and choose to find a reason to smile when they fall apart. In these moments, grace invites us to release our grip on our schedules, our expectations, and our perfectly made plans. In fact, by his grace, God uses these detours to transform us in ways we cannot transform ourselves. Every time we loosen our clenched fists and receive life's detours with open hands, God's grace transforms us into the image of his Son. Frustrating and disappointing moments are his vessels of grace, and he intends to use them to soften us, slow us down, and set us free from idols like control and perfectionism.

I've been learning to respond to life's detours with a three-word question: "Now what, God?"

The library is closed. "Now what, God?"

The dream I was chasing just went up in smoke. "Now what, God?"

The book deal I was working on just fell through. "Now what, God?"

I'm learning that a "Now What" mindset helps me move from disappointment to hopeful expectation.

The detour you're facing might be bigger than a closed library. Maybe you lost your job, your marriage, or your ministry. Today, let me gently remind you that God is sovereign over everything from closed libraries to shattered dreams. When life falls to pieces, God invites you to lean into grace and ask, "Now what, God?" His plans for you are good. They are filled with hope (Jeremiah 29:11). Step forward with hopeful expectations, and his grace will carry you through the most frustrating and disappointing circumstances.

Kay Warren captures this open-handed way of living in her book *Choose Joy*, where she writes, "Joy is the settled assurance that God is in control of all the details of my life, the quiet confidence that ultimately everything is going to be all right, and the determined choice to praise God in all things."[1] I want to live with this quiet confidence.

Creating Space for Whimsy

The week after the banana-peel incident, wet weather settles over western Pennsylvania, and a week of constant rain pushes us inside. Three days into the rainy weather, the walls are closing in, and the routines of our days begin to feel painfully monotonous. The voice of self-effort tells me this would be a good time to focus on the kids' academic skills.

I'm marking off pages for Bekah to complete in her summer reading workbook when a stray thought floats through my mind. My friend Beth has been talking about making more room for fun in her life lately. She's been talking about creating space for whimsy, and every time she talks this way, a tiny flame inside me begins to burn a little brighter.

The *Cambridge English Dictionary* defines whimsy as a "sudden wish or idea, especially one that cannot be reasonably explained."[2] Whimsy is fun, playful, eccentric, silly, and amusing.

As I sit at the table, I ask the Lord how we might add more playful fun to another long day.

Rain patters gently against the window—warm, summer rain.

Immediately, I see an invitation to step into the whimsy I crave. As the raindrops hang like glass beads from the poplar tree, I put baby Aiden safely in his crib to nap, place the baby monitor on the porch, call the older two children, and tell them we're heading outside.

"But it's raining," Bekah declares.

"Let's play in the rain," I say.

Both children look at me as if I've lost my mind.

"It'll be fun," I say as I slip out the door in my bare feet and stand with open arms as heaven unleashes a downpour.

Within minutes, we're chasing each other around the yard, pretending we're dragons, and laughing hysterically as we slip and slide through the mud puddles. It's messy. It's hilarious. It's the most playful moment I've had in months.

I didn't realize I needed a break to chase whimsy, but I did. I needed silliness. I needed to step away from the demands of my everyday life and have fun.

You might not realize it, but you need this too. I wonder how your life would change if you created more space for whimsy—if you went to the park with a Frisbee and your two closest friends, pulled the kite from the back of the closet, blew bubbles on a summer evening, or built a snowman?

Most likely, the shift into playfulness won't feel comfortable at first. You might wonder if you're wasting time and question whether God will bring fruit from the silliness. However, the decision to cultivate joy *will* bear good fruit. In an article titled, "Joy Changes Everything," Jim Wilder wrote, "Joy makes eyes sparkle and bonds form."[3]

We all need places to step away from the stress of everyday life and cultivate joy. The voice of self-effort tells us there's no time for such frivolity. God's grace offers a different invitation: Enjoy this life he's given you. Do things you love. Don't get so caught up on perfectly executing your plans that you forget to belly-laugh, lick ice cream cones, and gallop through rain showers. God is not calling us to huff and puff as we live on mission for him. Instead, he is pleased when we overflow with his joy.

Within the context of these moments, God does within us a work we cannot do for ourselves. He pushes out the grumpiness, softens us, and helps us take ourselves less seriously.

Questions for Reflection and Discussion:

1. In which area of your life do you get most bent out of shape when your plans don't work out? How do you typically respond?

2. How do you typically respond to "banana-peel" moments in your life? What is God showing you about loosening up and taking yourself less seriously?

3. Do you ever huff and puff around your home or workplace as you show everyone just how busy and important you are? What emotional rewards are you gaining from these behaviors? What might happen if you exchanged your stressed-out attitude for a light-hearted and joyful attitude?

4. Do you struggle with the cyclic nature of your life in any particular area? How might creating more space for whimsy help you appreciate the same faces and same spaces that fill your days?

5. Take some time to brainstorm a list of whimsical activities that would bring enjoyment to your life. What practical steps can you take today to incorporate more fun into your weekly or monthly routines and rhythms?

6. Is there anyone in your life who would enjoy a whimsical experience with you? Sometime in the next week, invite your children, your spouse, a sibling, a parent, a roommate, a coworker, or a close friend to pursue a whimsical activity with you. The secret is to choose something you will love, and then go enjoy it. Write about it in a journal or the space provided here afterward.

Notes:

1. Warren, K. (2020). *Choose joy : because happiness isn't enough*. Revell, A Division Of Baker Publishing Group.

2. *whimsy. (n.d.). Dictionary.cambridge.org.*
https://dictionary.cambridge.org/dictionary/english/whimsy

3. Wilder, J. (n.d.). *CONVERSATIONSJOURNAL.COM CHANGES EVERYTHING*. https://lifemodelworks.org/wp-content/uploads/2018/08/Joy-Changes-Everything.pdf

5

Grace for the Daily Grind:

Scrubbing Toilets with a Joyful Heart

Grace Takeaway: We lean into grace when we learn to let God transform our hearts through the humbling and hidden work he places before us.

A thread of silver water twists its way through an ochre stand of hardwoods as dusk exhales its first drowsy breath. I've found an hour to walk through the woods with a friend tonight, and our time together is a gift.

We talk about the books we've been reading, a recent conference at our church, and the way the daily grind sometimes wears on us.

"I'm trying to catch myself when I start Angry Cleaning and ask the Lord to change my heart," my friend confesses.

I've never heard the phrase, "Angry Cleaning," but she doesn't have to explain. I've Angry Cleaned more times than I can count.

My heart fills with compassion toward my friend as she shares her battle with this resentful mentality. At the heart of the matter, she wants more help from her husband, but he rarely extends the help she desires. She ends up taking on most of the household duties, and she has to fight to avoid becoming bitter about her circumstances. We talk about this as we stroll beneath the towering beech trees, and I try to encourage her. The conversation also prompts me to pay more attention to my own anger.

As I reflect on our conversation the day after our walk, I catch myself grumbling about the volume of dirty laundry our family produces every day. Later in the day, I catch myself complaining as I clean up the toys and blankets strewn throughout the living room.

I don't like the way resentment builds within me in these moments. I want to be the kind of woman who undertakes her daily work with a joyful heart, but I'm not sure how to make the shift.

Throughout the weeks following my friend's admission to Angry Cleaning, I began discussing the concept with more of my friends to see if they could relate. My informal survey revealed that most people approach at least one daily task with anger, bitterness, self-pity, or resentment.

For some of us, it's cleaning. For others, it's taking out the garbage, cooking all of the family's meals, mowing the lawn, raking the leaves, or taking out the dog. Most of the time, we aren't angry because we dislike the work. Instead, we feel like we're doing more work than others, or we're doing work that ought to belong to our family members or roommates. We undertake these tasks angrily because we feel unappreciated and even used. As a result, bitterness takes root in our hearts.

Today we're going to have an honest conversation about the daily grind. The daily grind is the hard, humble, and hidden work that fills our days. It's swishing toilets, washing dishes, folding laundry, paying bills, and completing the cyclic and mundane parts of our jobs. Your daily grind might include caring for young children, tending to the needs of a spouse who has chronic health issues, or serving as a caretaker for an elderly or disabled relative.

The daily grind is the work that isn't applauded by others. As we undertake this work, we often feel unacknowledged and unseen by our spouses, kids, coworkers, bosses, or whomever we've been called to serve. We feel like we are expected to lay down our lives as we meet the needs of those surrounding us, and we're tired.

It's easy to succumb to resentment amid this work; however, our loving heavenly Father has a different invitation for us. He invites us to lean into his grace and let him replace resentment with joy as we undertake the tiresome work that fills our days. I've been drawing near to God and asking him to transform my heart in this area, and I've discovered several life-changing insights that are helping me shift from grumbling to joy in this daily work: spending time in the secret place with Jesus; remembering the One I serve; and refusing to feel sorry for myself.

I invite you to join me as I share a replenishing part of my evening routine, and we'll begin by talking about letting Jesus affirm our work as a first step toward greater joy in the grind.

Spending Time in the Secret Place

Before I go to sleep at night, I often ask Jesus to search my heart and help me process any residual negative emotions from the day. Sometimes, he shows me sadness, and I grieve in his presence. At other times, I notice fear, worry, or anxiety, and he helps me relinquish my fears and plant my feet on his truth. Occasionally, he reveals resentment or anger from a moment when I felt like a loved one didn't care about me, see me, help me, or thank me.

When I recognize anger or resentment, I ask Jesus what he wants me to know about the situation. Sometimes, he shows me that I should have asked for help instead of embracing self-pity as I sought validation.

If he convicts me of a sinful attitude—such as self-pity—I confess it, repent, and ask him to change my heart. I then ask him to show me how he feels about the work that went unappreciated by others. Most of the time, he responds with a gentle impression that settles over me and draws me deeper into his love.

For example, years ago, my work as a special education teacher was ofter physically and emotionally exhausting. Managing a Life Skills Support classroom is tiresome work, and I often felt like I was spending all of my time putting out fires and very little time teaching.

During my last year in the classroom, one particular student was rarely compliant and responded to my directives by yelling at me. Several months into the school year, I went to see my doctor and told him about the chest pains I'd been experiencing.

After a thorough examination, my doctor assured me that I wasn't on the brink of a heart attack. He then asked if I'd been experiencing any extra stress that could be causing anxiety. I told him about the challenging student, and he encouraged me to find ways to release the stress that accumulated in my body throughout the trying days.

In the weeks following the appointment, I started taking walks outside on my lunch break to relieve stress. I learned to talk about my frustrations with supportive coworkers and tried to give thanks for the many gifts surrounding me at work. I also learned to draw close to Jesus and let him affirm my efforts in the classroom.

One day in the middle of the school year, I decided to keep track of how many times my difficult student yelled at me. By the end of the day, I had recorded 136 tally marks.

Crashing into bed at the end of that day, I poured my heart out to the Lord. "Lord, I'm not sure how much longer I can endure this stress," I told Jesus. "Show me what you want me to know."

Jesus didn't answer in an audible voice or even give me a clear thought. Instead, I had a deep sense of his love for my student. I also perceived that he was pleased with my efforts to remain calm and exude the kindness and compassion my student desperately needed.

I didn't wake up the next morning with a miraculous spring in my step or an entirely new perspective on the situation. It was still difficult. However, Jesus' affirmation helped me persevere through the difficult year. Every night, I returned to his arms and let him comfort me while his love and affirmation washed over me.

Learning to find our affirmation in Christ is vital because we will all face situations in which no one thanks us for our labor. Some husbands never thank their wives for the meals they cook, their endless household work, or the ways they sacrifice to earn extra income outside of the home. Some elderly parents consistently expect their adult children to meet all of their needs and then deride them for doing it wrong. Many bosses are critical, demanding, and not at all encouraging.

When others fail to thank us, help us, or acknowledge us, it hurts. It's easy to allow bitterness to take root in our hearts. I've learned that the single most powerful way to resist bitterness is to meet with Jesus and let him affirm my work.

Jesus wants you to bring him your emotions, too. Most of us will face moments when we feel worn down by our daily work— moments when we're tempted to Angry Clean, Angry Cook, or Angry Serve.

Establish a habit of bringing your emotions to Jesus at the end of each day. Let him search your heart and show you if you're embracing anger or resentment. Let him speak his love over you, fill your heart with self-sacrificing love for those he has called you to serve, and fill you with his joy.

No act of service goes unseen by the Lord. He is delighted when you humbly serve others for his sake. He sees every sacrifice you make, and he counts it as if you're directly serving him.

Here are a few of Jesus' words about the delight he experiences when we serve others:

> "Greater love has no one than this, that a person will lay down his life for his friends" (John 15:13).

> "But the greatest of you shall be your servant" (Matthew 23:11).

> "Take care not to practice your righteousness in the sight of people, to be noticed by them; otherwise you have no reward with your Father who is in heaven" (Matthew 6:1).

> "And the King will answer and say to them, 'Truly I say to you, to the extent that you did it for one of the least of these brothers or sisters of Mine, you did it for Me'" (Matthew 25:40).

Jesus' words in Matthew 25:40 remind us that when we serve ungrateful people, he counts it as if we are directly serving him. Let's focus on this verse as a segway into our second way of shifting from grumbling to joy: learning to serve others as if we are directly serving Jesus.

Remembering the One You Are Serving

Before we had children, my husband and I traveled to Guatemala to stay with a family of international workers and share the love of Christ with the people of Guatemala. During that time, I often meditated on Jesus' words: "Truly I tell you, whatever you did for one of the least of these brothers and sisters of mine, you did for me" (Matthew 25:40, NIV).

After returning home from Guatemala, I filled our home with photographs of indigenous Guatemalan children in colorful clothing. I didn't want to forget God's calling to share his love with "the least of these." I hung the photos to remind myself that Jesus calls me to love others—especially those who are often marginalized and overlooked—wherever I go.

Shortly after Bekah, our first child, was born, I remember rocking her through the long hours of a sleepless night. A pale moon peered through the frosted windowpane and cast shadows on the wall, and my gaze fell upon a photo of one of the Guatemalan children.

I remembered our time in Guatemala, and in many ways, the work of ministering to "the least of these" on the mountainsides of that distant land felt far more important—more spiritual— than the work of motherhood. A pang of longing filled my heart. I longed to return to the people of Guatemala and continue doing God's work.

As I sat with my longing, God imprinted the following words upon my heart: *Your children are "the least of these."*

We only had one child at the time, but I knew God was showing me that my role as a mother—to Bekah and to the children who would come after her—was my ministry to "the least of these." He was also showing me that whatever I do for my children, I do for Jesus.

Throughout the years since that moment, I've reminded myself of the truth God spoke to my heart hundreds of times. This truth changes the way I see the quiet and humble work that fills my days.

God uses this truth to help me imagine that I am directly serving Jesus when I care for my loved ones. For example, when my child won't stop asking questions from the backseat of the car, I imagine I am Jesus' mother, Mary. I remind myself to respond to my child the way I would respond if I were Mary, and he were young Jesus—asking 300 questions per day.

When a little one is awake all night with the stomach bug, when a child's twisted ankle requires me to carry him a mile out of the woods, or when serving my husband feels difficult, I imagine I am directly tending to Jesus' intimate needs.

Perhaps this sounds like an elementary idea, but I encourage you to give it a try. When you feel frustrated or annoyed by the people God has called you to love and serve, literally imagine you are serving Jesus. I'm not talking about a theoretical idea.

Visualize Jesus chatting nonstop from the backseat of your car or throwing his wet towel on the bedroom floor. Visualize the expression of joy on his face when you offer kindness to him.

I've found that when I remember I'm serving Jesus, I'm more patient, compassionate, and kind. I'm also far less likely to embrace self-pitying thoughts.

This leads to the third insight that helps me lean into grace in the daily grind: refusing to feel sorry for myself.

Refusing to Feel Sorry for Ourselves

The evening my friend confessed to Angry Cleaning, we had an honest conversation to see what was beneath her anger. At the heart of the matter, we discovered that she Angry Cleans because she feels like her husband doesn't care about her. He regularly leaves messes for her to clean up and plays video games for hours while she works. Her requests for help around the house always turn into arguments, and she's stopped asking for his help.

I'm blessed to have a caring husband who thanks me for my work and reminds our kids to thank me on a daily basis. He works outside the home full-time but still supports me and helps around the house. Many women are not so blessed.

Sadly, even with a considerate and thoughtful spouse, I can fall into the trap of feeling sorry for myself. When we were first adjusting to parenthood, I often felt envious of his freedom to leave the house, sleep through the night without interruptions, and leave the state for long hunting trips.

At times, I compared our roles and embraced self-pity. He would come home from a long hunting trip, and I'd spend the next 24 hours stomping around the house making a display of my hard work. He responded by treading lightly in my presence. I'm not proud to admit this, but playing the victim felt emotionally rewarding after long days of parenting without his help.

We continued in this pattern for several years. Finally, after one of his trips, God convicted me of self-pity. Tearfully, I told my husband how I was feeling. We talked about ways to support each other, shared our hearts, and worked through the problem together. He still hunts, but he no longer leaves home for more than a weekend. We're no longer divided on the issue.

Since that experience, I've learned that embracing self-pity only leads to bitterness. I've learned to catch myself when a victim mentality creeps in. The moment I recognize these thoughts and attitudes, I confess them to God, repent, and ask God to change my heart.

The Lord often reminds me that he is calling me to a higher realm of living. He is calling me to serve others out of love and devotion to Christ. He leads me into the secret place, affirms my work, and reminds me that those who work for the applause of others forfeit their reward from him (Matthew 6:1).

The people closest to us might never thank us for much of the obscure work that fills our days—work like changing toilet paper rolls, swishing toilets, and filling empty soap dishes. Most of this work will go unseen and unrecognized. However, as we complete these humble tasks, we can shift from resentment to joy purely for the sake of blessing others and knowing Jesus is pleased. This is the precise space where our hearts are molded to look like Jesus' heart of love.

I don't always get it right. I still grumble and stomp around the house at times, but I am growing. I'm also learning to catch myself when my attitude goes off the rails.

Additionally, I've learned to ask for help. When we are drowning in the demands of our days, there is a time to approach others in humility and ask for help. Often, vulnerably admitting that we need help leads to intimacy and connection, which help us guard our hearts against bitterness.

At other times, we are met with resistance, defensiveness, or even anger. In these instances, we can fall back on the principle we discussed at the beginning of the chapter: We serve others and offer self-sacrificing love for Jesus' sake.

A Final Word for the One Who Feels Dismissed

Before we wrap up this chapter, I want to take a moment to encourage every person who feels unseen and unappreciated in life's daily grind. I'm blessed with a godly husband who cares about my needs and loves me selflessly. Your situation might be vastly different.

You might be married to someone who expects your selfless service, never thanks you, and hardly seems to notice your efforts. Maybe you're the caretaker for an ungrateful relative or a disabled child who cannot express gratitude.

Dear friend, I have not walked in your shoes, and I don't claim to understand what your life is like, but I want you to know that my heart aches for you. God has not missed a moment of your service. Your selfless labor fills his heart with delight. Every time you serve your loved one, the Lord experiences your kindness as if you are serving him directly.

Your loved one might never thank you or express a hint of concern about your feelings. Nothing about this is fair, and continuing to give under these circumstances is a test of faithfulness. However, God is leading you to maturity as you learn to do this work for him alone. Not a single ounce of your energy is wasted.

Often, we think of grace as a gift requiring no effort on our part. This is where we need to return to our definition of grace: When God works in our lives to accomplish what we cannot do for ourselves.

We cannot transform our hearts to look more like Jesus' heart of love. Only God can do this work within us. However, we do have a role. Our role is to obey. Obedience includes doing the work God sets in front of us with grateful, joyful hearts. As we practice cultivating gratitude and finding joy in serving others for Jesus' sake, God wi l mold our hearts to look more like Jesus' heart of love.

Questions for Reflection and Discussion:

1. Ask God to show you if you have been feeling sorry for yourself in any area of your life. What is he revealing to you? Name something for which you can give thanks the next time self-pity creeps into your mind.

2. Name someone in your life who serves others with love and humility. What characteristics might you imitate as you aim to lean into grace and serve without grumbling?

3. God showed me that my children are "the least of these" in this season of my life. Who are the "least of these"—the people God has called you to humbly serve—in this season of your life?

4. Name a recurring situation in your life in which it would be helpful to imagine you are directly serving Jesus. In what ways would your responses be different if Jesus were the one you were serving?   Ask the Lord to change your perspective as you remember that you *are* serving Jesus in these moments.

5. Do you ever resist asking for help because you're embracing the emotional benefits of playing the victim?   Describe the situations in which this happens in your life and share whatever God is revealing to you.

6

Grace for Wonder Woman Syndrome:

Resisting the Urge to Be the Hero

Grace Takeaway: We lean into grace when we stop trying to be everything to everyone and embrace our actual lives.

Dawn trickles through burgundy curtain panels as I place my baby boy in his crib. He just nursed for the ninth time of the night, and to say I'm exhausted would be a vast understatement. Crashing into bed, I pray for another hour of sleep and pull the comforter over my head. It's Sunday—a day for resting.

I've almost found sleep when I hear the bedroom door creak open. I don't move. If I don't move, maybe the intruder won't know I'm here.

"Mom, I can't open my lollipop," my little boy's voice announces.

"You should be in bed, not eating lollipops," I snap.

"I couldn't sleep." he protests. I'm too tired to explain that lollipops don't generally cure insomnia, and I open the wrapper and send him back downstairs.

Twenty minutes later, it's clear that my body has no intentions of returning to sleep, and I stumble from the dark bedroom. Much to my surprise, I'm immediately greeted by a white bunny. We don't have any free-roaming pets living in our house, which makes this a disheveling surprise. Peanut, our tame bunny, is visiting from her permanent residence outside and sits nervously at the top of the steps.

Shuffling past Peanut, I make my way downstairs and discover Bekah sitting on the couch holding a different rabbit. This one is a tiny wild rabbit, and the bunny is wrapped in a blanket on her lap. "Look at what Daddy found outside! It was lost and can't find its mommy's nest!" she exclaims.

"Wow," I reply in the most cheerful voice I can muster.

Caleb continues to chat about lollipops as I make my way to the kitchen, where my precious husband is making breakfast. He sees me coming and prudently scuttles out of the path between me and the coffeepot.

"Mom, we need to find the baby bunny's nest and return it to its mother!" Bekah calls from the living room.

"Can you put a cartoon on for me?" Caleb whines.

Baby Aiden squawks through the monitor.

A gunshot sounds from the dining room. (You can't make this stuff up.) My husband has abandoned his cooking project and is now propped against the open back door as he shoots at something in the backyard.

This is my life. This is what a "restful" Sunday morning looks like.

Sadly, the first hour of the day continues to be anything but restful as I put together a Crock-Pot meal for a friend, throw a batch of cookies in the oven for an event a different friend is hosting, and tend to the immediate needs of my family. An hour later, I finally lock myself in my bedroom with a Bible and a cold cup of coffee.

Defining Wonder Woman Syndrome

I'm sipping the cold coffee and staring blankly at the open Bible on my lap when I come to a startling realization: Trying to be everything for everyone in every moment is stealing my joy.

I've spent most of my life embracing the notion that I can say yes to every need surrounding me and be the hero for everyone in my life. I first recognized this mentality serval months after my wedding day. I noticed a book on my husband's dresser called *I Married Wonder Woman . . . Now What?* I didn't think much of it at the time. I loved feeling helpful and needed, and I saw no issue with being compared to Wonder Woman.

However, in the years that followed, the Lord began showing me that Wonder Woman Syndrome was not leading me into the life I desired. Wonder Woman Syndrome (feel free to use the phrase Superman Syndrome throughout the remainder of this chapter if you are a man) is fueled by the deep belief that I can be everything to everyone in my life. I feel compelled to say yes to every friend's request for assistance; I rarely set boundaries and don't ask for help. As a result, I find myself emotionally and physically exhausted.

Wonder Woman Syndrome is sometimes related to the fear of failure, as we discussed in Chapter Three; however, it is often motivated by sincere love. Because we love our families and friends, we want to meet their needs. Sadly, aiming to be the hero in every situation that presents itself leads to burnout and exhaustion.

Today, I invite you to join me as I share two insights the Lord has been teaching me about avoiding Wonder Woman Syndrome. He is teaching me to embrace the reality of my actual life, and he regularly reminds me to slow down and savor his good gifts.

Embracing the Reality of Your Actual Life

The week after the free-roaming bunny incident, I told a friend how burned out I was feeling.

"I feel guilty for even admitting that I'm so worn out. After all, this is the life I wanted for myself. Many women would give anything for this life with a loving husband and three beautiful children. Admitting that I'm exhausted and burned out feels ungrateful," I confessed.

"Stacey, admitting that you're feeling burned out isn't the same as ingratitude," my friend gently responded. "Instead of shaming yourself for feeling this weary, what would it look like to be compassionate toward yourself? What would it look like to extend grace to yourself in this season?"

I knew my friend was onto something and spent a few days wrestling with her words. *What would it look like to extend grace to myself?*

One warm summer evening as I watched a golden sun sink behind the hills, I sensed the Lord inviting me to pray a new prayer.

The simple prayer went like this: "Lord, help me to accept the reality of my *actual* life."

As I spoke the words of this prayer for the first time, I immediately felt as if a weight had been lifted from my shoulders. I recognized that I'd been chasing the ideals of a perfect home and flourishing writing career while also caring for a newborn, recovering from major abdominal surgery, and tending to an eight-year-old and a four-year-old.

I was floundering because I was chasing the *ideal* image of a life I had created in my mind. It wasn't the *actual* life God had set before me or the life he was calling me to live.

Baby Aiden lay asleep in a sling on my chest as I wrote the following words in my journal:

> *Lord, help me accept the reality of my actual life. My reality is that I will not accomplish much more than caring for this baby in this season of life. I can fight this reality and become stressed as I try to impose my agenda. Or I can humbly accept the reality of my life now and embrace these moments of caring for this little one and doing little else. This is the schedule you have for me right now. My responsibility is to be humble enough to surrender to the reality of my actual life.*

I've asked the Lord to help me accept the reality of my life hundreds, if not thousands, of times since that summer day. This simple prayer can be a turning point every time we catch ourselves hustling and hurrying in pursuit of unrealistic ideals.

As I reflect on my life, I recognize that many of my burned-out seasons took place during times when I was trying to force my agenda and accomplish more than God was asking of me. However, when I ask God to help me accept my *actual* life, his grace meets me. I realize he is providing everything I need to do the work *he* has placed in front of me.

Accepting the reality of your life might mean you need to step back from a few commitments, settle for imperfection at work, or leave the dishes n the sink overnight. Perhaps God is asking you to pour your whole heart into one all-consuming task and leave everything else for a different season.

Ask God to help you embrace the reality of your actual life and be brave enough to follow wherever you sense he is leading. As you embrace this reality, remind yourself that God is not calling you to be everything to everyone at all times. As you learn to lay down this desire to be the hero in every situation in your life, you might soon discover that living within the margins God has set for you leads to the replenishment you've been craving.

I encourage you to set aside some time to talk to God about your weariness and any sense of burnout in your life. Ask him to show you what it would look like to slow down and embrace the reality of your actual life.

After you've talked with him, I invite you to return with me to the day of little Aiden's long-awaited appointment with the pediatric cardiologist. I'm sharing this story in a chapter devoted to Wonder Woman Syndrome because Aiden's appointment led me to a perspective that regularly helps me lean into grace and resist the urge to be the hero. I pray these words help you lean into God's grace, too.

Learning to Savor God's Gifts

Aiden's appointment falls on a gorgeous summer morning with clear skies and a sense of hope rising with the sun. Because we are unsure of what the future holds, my husband decides to save his vacation days for future appointments. My parents watch the older two children, and I make the long drive to visit the specialist with our beautiful baby boy.

After arriving at the office, I wait for the doctor to call us into the small examination room, and I remind myself of my fear-fighting Bible verse: "All the days ordained for this little boy's life are already written" (Psalm 139:16).

The words have barely left my lips when the nurse opens the door and kindly says, "We're ready for you."

With unsteady hands, I undress our precious little one. He fusses and squirms, and my body is tense with nervous energy.

"Lord, I need you," I pray silently.

Immediately, I remember singing my fear-fighting worship song, "Raise a Hallelujah," as the doctor examined little Aiden's heart in my womb months ago.

As I gently remove his onesie, I begin humming our song—like an anthem reminding me that we will praise God no matter what.

After placing Aiden on the examining table, the most surprising event takes place. Instead of screaming and flailing, he closes his eyes, turns his head to the side, and drifts off to sleep. As any mother of a newborn knows, this is its own version of a miracle.

Watching our boy sleep, I sense God's kindness and his presence as he pours out his grace—stilling my soul and inviting me to trust him. In the darkness of the tiny room, God does a work I cannot do in my strength: He shrouds me with the peace that surpasses understanding.

As the doctor uses the ultrasound machine to capture images of Aiden's heart, I rest assured that I can trust the One who knit his heart together inside my womb.

After a few minutes spent capturing images, the doctor turns on the light, looks into my eyes, and speaks words I will never forget: "His heart is perfectly healthy and normal. The defect is gone!" My eyes fill with tears as I pull my little one close and thank God for his healing.

The next morning, I reflect on God's goodness as I sit by the window and watch a scrim of fair-weather clouds arise from the western skyline. My heart is filled with thanksgiving for the gift of Aiden's life.

I allow myself to ponder everything I love about this baby who will most likely be our last child. I reflect on the fulfillment I find when I care for his needs—comforting him in the night, providing him nourishment, wearing him in the sling as we join his older siblings for adventures in the woods, and bathing his tiny body with sweet smelling soap in the plastic baby bathtub.

The moment of gratitude nourishes my soul deeply, and I spend a few moments reflecting on everything I appreciate about the older two children as well.

When my quiet time at the window draws to a close, I feel replenished and grateful for the gift of my life. Moving into the day with this mindset, I realize that the intentional shift into gratitude helps me become more fully present in my moments as they unfold in front of me.

I leave my phone inside the house and take the kids outside for bubble-blowing, bike riding, and castle-building in the sandbox. We spend hours chasing bubbles, driving toy trucks through the sand, and sitting in the shade.

I don't accomplish much that can be measured. I don't knock out my to-do list, write thank-you notes, cook dinner, or sweep the floor. However, I am fully present with my kids. My heart overflows with joy as we belly-laugh over our backyard playfulness. This is the life I desire. It's a life in which I take time to savor God's goodness in the quiet moments and slow down to enjoy his gifts when I'm living in the less tranquil moments.

As you aim to move away from Wonder Woman Syndrome, taking the time to savor God's gifts can refresh your soul and help you become more present within your moments, too. Finding just a few minutes to name and give thanks for God's gifts each morning prepares your heart and mind to watch his gifts unfold throughout the remainder of the day.

I'll offer deeper insights into my morning routine in Chapter Eleven; for today, I invite you to begin a new routine of starting your days by savoring God's gifts. Before you get out of bed each morning—or while you drive to work or eat breakfast—take a few moments to consider everything you love about one or two of God's blessings in your life. Try to choose a different gift every day. You might thank God for different people, your pets, joyful moments, or anything that feels like a blessing to you. I'd also like to note that quickly listing as many gifts as we can think of is different from savoring the gifts.

Listing God's gifts can be helpful, but slowing down and taking the time to deeply appreciate just one or two blessings offers a much greater shift in my soul. Not surprisingly, recent discoveries about the function of the brain reveal that appreciation calms the nervous system and enables us to connect with God and others.[1] By cultivating gratitude in the early morning hours, I prepare my mind to notice God's gifts throughout my days. I also prepare myself to put people above tasks, which is essential if I'm going to resist the urge to be Wonder Woman.

I pray my words will help you find refreshment and also help you notice when you are slipping into Wonder Woman Syndrome. God has not asked us to be everything for everyone in our lives.

A Final Note About Answered Prayers

As I reflect on this chapter, I feel compelled to pause with you for a moment, dear reader. I hesitated to share the story of Aiden's healed heart in this chapter because I'm aware that our story could have played out differently. Perhaps your difficult story didn't end with a family celebration and a morning spent basking in God's restorative goodness.

I want you to know that I see you. More importantly, God sees you. I shared my story because God used it to help me grow in gratefulness and become more present with my family, but I know this is not every person's story.

I want you to know that I have walked through the deep waters of grief and heartbreak as well. Often, I have not walked well. At times, I've turned away from God in offense. However, God is using my life experiences to teach me that regardless of how the stories of my life play out, soaking in his goodness always brings healing and hope. Focusing on God's gifts consistently pulls me out of Wonder Woman Mode, but it also helps me fix my gaze on Jesus when life threatens to drown me.

We all need this shift from time to time. Whether we've run ourselves ragged trying to be superheroes or whether we're walking through the deep waters of grief and loss, we need our loving Father to lift our heads. Throughout my four decades on this green earth, I've found no discipline more powerful than learning to soak in God's goodness. With all the tenderness in my heart, I invite you to turn toward the Lord and savor what is good in your life today. The Lord will not waste your sacrifice of thanksgiving.

Questions for Reflection and Discussion:

1. In what ways do you wrestle with Wonder Woman Syndrome? What are the physical, emotional, spiritual, and mental results of trying to be the hero for too many people?

2. On a scale of 1 to 10, how stressed do you feel right now (1 being the lowest and 10 being the highest)? Ask God to show you the biggest stressors in your life, and list them here as a practice in awareness.

3. What did God show you about accepting the reality of your actual life? In which realm of your life do you need to stop chasing your ideals and accept God's assignment for you?

4. Would you describe your life as restful and peace-filled? Why or why not?

5. Spend a few moments savoring one of God's gifts. Try to engage all five senses as you consider everything you love about this gift. What shifts do you notice in your emotions, mind, and body after a few minutes spent relishing this gift?

Notes:

1. Wilder, J., & Willard, D. (2020). *Renovated : God, Dallas Willard & the church that transforms*. Navpress.

7

Grace for Spiritual Boredom:

Doing What You Love *with* Jesus

Grace Takeaway: We lean into grace when we overcome spiritual boredom by making time to pursue our passions and enjoy our favorite pastimes with Jesus.

I was in my early twenties when I surrendered my life to Christ and committed to growing in my relationship with him. As I began seeking God, I discovered the power of spiritual disciplines for connecting with him in deeper ways. The traditional Christian disciplines—prayer, Bible reading, worship, silence, solitude, and fasting—became catalysts for a thriving relationship with the Lord.

Since that time, these practices have transformed my spiritual life by leading me closer to God. I've discovered that these disciplines enable me to experience God's peace in stressful seasons, and they lead me into his healing arms in times of loss. Additionally, over the past two decades, God has drastically changed the way I see the world as a result of my interaction with his written Word, including Bible study, reading, and memorization.

I've flourished when seeking God through these methods in some seasons; however, at other times, I've struggled with a sense of feeling disconnected from him. Some days, I feel frustrated because I read entire chapters of my Bible without comprehending a single word. I've also been known to make mental grocery lists during worship, and I often have a difficult time quieting my mind when I try to rest with God in silence and solitude. It's humbling to admit this to you, but there are times when I feel restless—and even bored—in my spiritual life.

I share this with you today because I know I'm not alone. We all experience highs and lows as we seek the Lord, and most believers experience spiritual emptiness or boredom at times.

This restlessness doesn't happen because there's something wrong or lacking within the traditional spiritual disciplines. These are powerful tools, and we need them. However, when they become routine and lifeless, finding fresh ways to connect with God is helpful.

We'll learn more about connecting with God through traditional disciplines in Chapter Eleven. Today, we're going to explore an additional discipline that can help us overcome spiritual dryness: pursuing our favorite activities with Jesus.

Your favorite activity or hobby can become a spiritual discipline when you learn to pursue it with Jesus. Jesus waits to reveal himself to you in new ways through this practice. In the meantime, the Lord will do something for you—something you cannot do for yourself—he will lead you deeper into a joyful, thriving relationship with himself.

It might feel far-fetched to suggest that your favorite pastime can be a spiritual discipline but stick with me as I share what this looked like in my life a few months after becoming the mother of three little ones. I'll share my journey, and then I'll invite you to consider what activity you might pursue as a spiritual discipline. We'll also explore practical ways to combine traditional spiritual disciplines with our favorite activities as life-giving avenues for encountering Jesus. First, I invite you to join me in the woods.

Do What You Love *with* Jesus

It's a brisk October evening, and the cobalt firmament shines brilliantly above autumn's ochre canopy. My hiking boots crunch over maple leaves scattered on a muddied trail. I snake through the towering hardwoods and carefully cross the log that leads toward Wolf Creek.

Reaching the grove of hemlocks where I will sit for the next hour, I pull the matches from my pocket and begin collecting twigs to kindle my fire.

Within a few minutes, the flames lick the branches in front of my feet, and I stretch out my hands to warm them over the fire. The smell of pine smoke wafts through the trees, and a red squirrel gnaws on a walnut nearby.

I feel vibrant and joyful—like some part of my soul has been stirred to life through the simple process of trekking through the woods and building a small campfire. Throughout my twenties, I often spent weeks backpacking through the wilderness and regularly connecting with the land in these ways. Now, with three children at home, this isn't a season for spending a week— or even a night—living in a tent.

I came to the woods tonight because I'm desperate to reconnect with Jesus in this space. I've been feeling spiritually empty, and I need to draw close to the Lord in a different way. Resting with him in a place where no one needs me—a place where I am free to set aside the many hats I wear—feels life-giving and even sacred. Slowing down to embrace the pastime of connecting with nature awakens something in the deepest part of me.

As the fire dances, I recall a different season in my life. It was a season spent exploring the far corners of the earth with everything I needed to survive shoved into a large backpack.

I learned to bathe in mountain streams and live on dehydrated meals cooked over my small camp stove. My tent became my home, and evening campfires kept me company.

Sitting by campfires and hiking through forests were routine parts of my life in those days, and I often took the necessary actions that went along with camping for granted. Within a few minutes, I could easily unpack my belongings, erect my tent, arrange my bedding, start a fire, and cook dinner.

I reflect on these routines as I sit beneath the hemlocks, and it occurs to me that nothing about this evening feels routine. Because it's been so long since I've built a fire in the woods, I'm mesmerized by everything about this experience—almost as if this is the first time I've ever hiked into a forest and spent an hour enjoying a campfire.

My senses are fully engaged with every part of this evening: the coolness of the air, the sound of my boots crunching over the leaves, and the tedious process of collecting and snapping the twigs for the fire. As I reflect on it, I search my vocabulary for a word to describe the way the process feels tonight. It feels mindful in a way that is unhurried, deliberate, and aware of God's presence with me. It feels *sacramental*.

As this word floats through my mind, I consider the way I take the Lord's Supper on Sunday mornings. I hold the tiny wafer between my fingers and feel its contours. I remember Christ's sacrifice on the cross and chew slowly as I allow the sacrament to help me reflect upon the profound spiritual reality that Christ came to dwell among us and paid the price for my sins on the cross. I am fully engaged and wholly present. I'm aware of Jesus' presence with me. I drink the tiny cup of grape juice with the same thoughtfulness and taste the tart fruit on my tongue with fully engaged senses. My mind and heart are open to the reality of Christ's sacrifice, and I sense his presence as I commune with him.

This particular evening in the woods, the posture of my heart feels surprisingly similar to the sacramental mindset I experience when taking communion. As I interact with the temporal world, I feel connected to Jesus in a way that is alert and honest. Hiking through the woods, starting the fire, and sitting here as the sun sinks behind the hills all feel like acts of worship. I sense Jesus' presence. I sense his delight in me, and my heart overflows with his joy.

I also find space to talk to him about everything that's been on my heart lately. I talk to him in the same way I would talk to a close friend. I tell him about my weariness, my dreams, my desires, and my longings.

As I imagine Jesus sitting with me beneath the hemlock trees, peace fills my heart. I feel replenished, grateful, and more alive than I've felt in months. The evening feels like a work of God's grace—a work I could not do within myself.

Enjoy Your Favorite Pastime with Jesus

As you read my words, perhaps a special hobby came to your mind. Maybe you love to paint, ride horses, golf, knit, or scrapbook. Perhaps you've neglected this pastime because your life is full, and you haven't made time for it. Possibly, you regularly enjoy this activity, but you've never slowed down to approach it with a sacramental mindset. You've never invited Jesus to join you as you enjoy it.

Today, I'd like to offer you an invitation: At some point in the next week, carve out an hour and use it to enjoy your favorite activity while communing with Jesus. You might dust off your sewing machine, pull out your video-making equipment, find your acrylics or your sketchpad, write poetry, or get out your cross-stitching. If you enjoy baking and cooking, try a new recipe or create your own. If you enjoy active outdoor activities, consider dusting off your skis, your kayak, or your bike.

Most importantly, invite Jesus to join you as you pursue this activity. Jesus is always with us; however, it's easy to go through the motions without being aware of his presence within us. Ask

Jesus to help you become more aware of his presence as you slowly enjoy your favorite pastime with him.

Also, take the time to allow all of your senses to become engaged with the physical elements in front of you. For example, if you are baking a cake, a sacramental mindset might include talking to Jesus while you arrange the measuring cups and carefully place the ingredients on the countertop. You might slowly combine the ingredients, marveling at the way they are transformed as you mix them. You then take your time pouring the batter into the pan and enjoying the aroma as it bakes. All the while, you thank the Lord for his provision. You are open to him as you allow him to impress his truth upon your heart. You are fully engaged and fully present in every way. The routine activity becomes holy—threaded with divine wonder. You enjoy creating alongside the Creator, and in the process, your love for him deepens. Your capacity for joy expands.

In an article titled "Everyday Life as a Sacrament," Ronald Rolheiser reminds us that because Jesus took on flesh, every physical element in our lives can potentially be approached with a holy, sacramental attitude.[1] Imagine the transformation we might experience if we learned to prepare and eat more of our meals, care for our bodies, clean our homes, and go about our everyday tasks with this perspective.

By regularly cultivating a sacramental mindset while pursuing activities we enjoy, we create new neuropathways. As a result, this mentality will carry over to other parts of our lives. We will become more aware of Jesus' presence with us while we're caring for our homes, driving down the road, going about our workdays, cooking dinner, and even watching the evening news. By learning to stay engaged with Jesus throughout our days, we can overcome spiritual boredom while also learning what it means to pray without ceasing.

I conclude this section of our chapter with Rolheiser's thoughts on learning to encounter Jesus in the ordinary realms of our lives—realms like cooking, painting, and exercising:

> For many reasons, each of us has the propensity to miss seeing God in the ordinary because we are forever searching for him in the extraordinary. We tend, nearly always, to miss the sacredness of the domestic as we look for the sacred in the monastic. Too often we are unaware that the incarnation fundamentally changed us from being theists to being Christians, that is, from being people who believe in God to becoming people who believe in a God who was made flesh in Christ.[2]

Because Christ came in the flesh and lived among us, we can encounter his presence amid all of the routines of our temporal lives. When this happens, our lives are transformed.

What About Traditional Spiritual Disciplines?

This invitation to pursue a favorite pastime with a sacramental mindset is not an incitement to give up on the traditional spiritual disciplines. Instead, it is an additional discipline to enhance our spiritual lives.

Furthermore, *combining* traditional spiritual disciplines with our favorite activities can help us become more aware of Jesus' presence with us. For example, we can cultivate a greater awareness of Jesus' presence by listening to worship music while painting, biking, or enjoying our favorite activities. Listening to Christian podcasts, online sermons, or audio Bibles while enjoying our hobbies can also help us stay focused on Jesus.

Throughout my twenties, I often carried notecards with me on hikes. I wrote Bible verses on these notecards and memorized dozens of verses while hiking through the hills of Pennsylvania. During the same season, I often went for morning jogs before going to work. My morning jogs became sacred spaces for prayer. I shared my cares and concerns with Jesus while I jogged, prayed for my students, and listened for his still small voice to direct my days.

In my current season of my life, a prayer board hangs beside our treadmill in the basement. The board is filled with photos of friends and family members, and I often pray for these loved ones while I walk on the treadmill. Other times, I watch my favorite Bible teachers online or listen to worship music while I exercise.

It's also important to note that a discipline is an activity that is repeatedly practiced. For this reason, I *consistently* create space to connect with Jesus in the outdoors. I don't always have time to build a campfire, but most days, I can find at least 15 minutes to walk in the woods behind our house and talk to Jesus. This restorative routine adds depth and joy to my relationship with the Lord.

I encourage you to look at your schedule and prioritize a time to enjoy your favorite activity with Jesus at least once a week, more often if possible. In doing so, you will add a new, revitalizing spiritual discipline to your life.

As you consider what it might look like to connect with Jesus over an enjoyable activity, I leave you with a question a mentor once asked me: "Are the disciplines you're using to encounter Jesus leading you into life-giving encounters with him? If not, what might he want you to do about that?"

Questions for Reflection and Discussion:

1. Describe your experience with traditional spiritual disciplines such as Bible reading, prayer, worship, and fasting. Are these disciplines currently life-giving for you? If not, what is God showing you? Where is he leading you?

2. What life-giving passion or hobby came to mind as you read about my hike and campfire? How might pursuing your pastime with a sacramental mindset deepen your relationship with the Lord?

3. After finding time to enjoy your pastime with the Lord, describe your experience. How was this experience different from the normal rhythms of your daily life?

4. Did God reveal anything noteworthy to you through this activity? Did you find any part of this experience particularly challenging or frustrating? How might you apply what you learned to other areas of your life?

5. What traditional spiritual discipline might you add to your favorite hobby to help you connect with Jesus while enjoying this activity? Try it and write about your experience.

Notes:

1. *Everyday Life as Sacrament | Ron Rolheiser*. (n.d.).
https://ronrolheiser.com/everyday-life-as-sacrament/#.YZgSPE7MLIW

2. *The Incarnation Means God is in the Ordinary | Ron Rolheiser.* (n.d.). https://ronrolheiser.com/the-incarnation-means-god-is-in-the-ordinary/#.Y-lKNHDMLIU

8

Grace for Overwhelming Moments:

Returning to Peace When Your Buttons Are Pushed

Grace Takeaway: We lean into grace when we learn to return to God's peace in overwhelming and frustrating circumstances.

As I sit to write this chapter, several weeks have passed since the Lord invited me to cultivate a sacramental mindset. I've been applying this mindset to more than just hiking. I've been baking Christmas cookies slowly and mindfully—enjoying each step of the process. I've been wrapping the children's presents with gratitude in my heart and talking to Jesus while I attach sparkling bows to colorful boxes. God is softening my heart and smoothing my rough edges on this journey into his grace.

A few days ago, the Lord provided another opportunity to lean into his grace while preparing for Christmas. What started as a peaceful afternoon spent searching for the perfect Christmas tree—all while cultivating a sacramental mindset—quickly shifted into an emotionally overwhelming evening. I invite you to join our family in the woods, and we'll talk about learning to return to God's peace when challenging situations push our buttons.

It's an unseasonably warm December afternoon as our family trudges to the top of the hill where scotch pines and blue spruces speckle the beige backdrop of weathered goldenrod. I am fully engaged and prayerful as the sun shines warm upon our skin and a brow of feathery cirrus clouds stretches across the western horizon.

As we scan the array of trees, we take time to imagine which tree will best fit in the corner of our living room. We finally agree on a short-needled spruce. After cutting it down, we head for home with grateful hearts.

A few hours later, the tree is settled in the corner of the living room, and it's time to dig out the ornaments and start decorating. I thoughtfully inhale the aroma of pine pitch and reflect on our wonderful afternoon in the woods. It's been a grace-filled day—unhurried and woven together with the golden thread of gratitude.

When Our Buttons Are Pushed

Before I tell you about the moment in which this glorious day fell apart, let's pause for a moment and talk about the moments when our "buttons are pushed." For the purpose of our conversation today, I'll use the term "trigger" to refer to the events and situations that push our buttons, causing us to feel upset and overwhelmed.

As you've probably noticed throughout the previous seven chapters, messes in our home are often triggers for me. I'm embarrassed to admit that I repeatedly lose my patience when the kids track mud into the house, dishes are left stacked in the living room, watermarks stain the couch cushions, and dirty fingerprints cover the walls.

Your triggers are probably different from mine. I invite you to consider what makes you come unraveled as I share the events that unfolded while my excited children "helped" decorate for Christmas.

The Unraveling

After hauling what feels like 45 boxes of decorations from the basement, the oldest children help me pull ornaments, tangled strings of lights, and Santa figurines from dusty boxes. I take a deep breath as they decorate the house according to their tastes, argue over decorations for their rooms, and prematurely cover the bottom half of the tree with ornaments.

"Breathe, Stacey," I whisper under my breath. "Just breathe. Enjoy this process. These kids will only be young for so long."

Meanwhile, stress hormones surge through my body, and the wise voice telling me to breathe is soon silenced by the chaos unfolding in front of me.

My diaphragm tightens as the kids bicker over where to place the decorations. As I break up the arguments and attempt to explain the importance of stringing the lights on the tree *before* hanging the ornaments, I feel my right eyelid twitching with stress. Tension rises as I attempt to figure out why the tangled web of lights won't illuminate. In the meantime, the pine needles and crumpled leaves scattered across the floor threaten to send me over the edge.

I reflect on my state of mind as the string of lights becomes increasingly tangled, and I realize that I desperately need God to help me protect my family from my overwhelming emotions.

Unlike me, decorating for Christmas might not push your buttons; nevertheless, I imagine you can relate to my emotional response amid our family's Christmas chaos. Maybe you mutter profanities when careless drivers cut you off in traffic, or you feel suffocated in large crowds. Perhaps you can't stand the stress of falling behind at work, or you go into fight or flight mode when dealing with conflict.

We talked about the long-term stress that leads to burnout in Chapter Six. Today, we'll explore a practical way to lean into God's grace when overwhelming *moments* send us into fight or flight mode. First, we'll talk about the way God designed our bodies to respond to crises. Then, I'll invite you to join me as I share a process that helps me return to peace in overwhelming moments. My prayer is that my process will help you return to peace as well.

God's Design for Crisis Situations

Let me begin this section by acknowledging that decorating for Christmas is not usually a crisis situation. Unfortunately, our central nervous systems don't always discern the difference between true crises and situations that are simply overwhelming and stressful.

In stressful moments, adrenaline surges through our bodies and sends us into fight or flight mode. In fight mode, a surge of stress hormones prepares us for battle. In flight mode, we feel the sudden compulsion to get as far away from the stressor as possible. This might include emotionally shutting down or physically withdrawing.[1]

It's important to note that these physiological responses aren't sinful. God designed our bodies to respond to stress by fighting or fleeing for our protection. Fighting an armed assailant or running from an angry predator are protective responses, and we don't need to feel ashamed when our bodies respond according to their God-given design. However, we all face moments when we feel shaken by circumstances that don't demand physical battles or rushed escapes. In these moments, learning how to de-escalate is the first step toward experiencing God's grace.

We're going to spend the remainder of this chapter exploring a three-step process to help our nervous systems move out of fight or flight mode and return to peace and joy.

Three Steps for Returning to Peace

I hesitate to break this de-escalation process into three steps because following God is never a formula. There's no step-by-step method for activating God's grace. God's grace is a free gift offered by a loving Father to his precious children. However, as we've been learning throughout our time together, we do play a role in positioning ourselves to receive God's grace.

God is always ready to impart his grace, and our role is to make sure we are available to receive it. This is at the heart of *leaning into grace*.

We can lean into God's grace in our triggered moments (when we are in fight or flight mode) by remembering the acrostic *CAT*. I'm moving into teaching mode a bit today, but I pray you'll stick with me. This method of calming my central nervous system so that I can connect with God has transformed my life, and I hope to offer you the same gift.

In the acrostic *CAT*, *C* stands for *Calm your nervous system*. The first step when stress hormones flood our bodies is to calm our central nervous systems. This is important because when we're triggered, we often lose the ability to connect with God and others. We need to be able to connect with God in order to move to the second step of the process. The second step of the process is to *Ask God why you're reacting the way you are*. This step includes bringing our raw emotions to God and processing them in his presence. Lastly, *T* stands for *Truth*. After talking to God about our emotions, the final step is to stand on God's Word of Truth instead of standing on our feelings. Let's review:

1. Calm your nervous system.

2. Ask God why you're reacting the way you are.

3. Stand on God's Truth instead of standing on your feelings.

I invite you to join me as I share the way this process unfolded during our Christmas decorating frenzy.

C: Calm Your Nervous System

Return with me to the living room where the boxes of Christmas decorations are strewn across the couches, pine pitch sticks to our socks, and my beloved husband has rescued me from the tangled strand of Christmas lights.

"Why don't you take your evening walk before it's dark?" my husband suggests as he finishes detangling the string of lights, plugs them in, and saves Christmas. Bless his heart.

I feel a bit embarrassed because I know he sees my undercurrent of stress, but I heed his gentle advice and head outside.

As I walk beneath the descending dusk, I breathe deeply. The measured breaths slow my hammering pulse and my racing mind. I'm not thinking about neuroscience as I stroll down our country road, but my walk is serving an important function. By stepping into a peaceful setting and focusing on my breathing, I am calming my central nervous system. I am also returning to relational mode.[2]

Relational mode is the state of mind in which we're able to connect with God and other people. Here are a few indicators that we've stepped out of relational mode: Other people feel like enemies; we want to lash out or withdraw; we feel irritated; and we have no capacity for relational connection.[3]

Does it ever feel like a switch has been flipped in your brain? When the switch is flipped, you're quick to react in anger or withdraw by shutting down emotionally. You're unable to connect relationally with other people or with God. Until the switch flips back to relational mode, connection is next to impossible.[4]

Calming our nervous systems helps us return to relational mode. This is a vital step in our triggered moments because we need to be in relational mode to hear from God. *God wants to show us what's beneath our emotions so that we can return to peace.*

Let's look at a few simple ways to calm our nervous systems and return to relational mode. These ideas are adapted from the teaching of Dr. Jim Wilder and his colleagues at Life Model Works as well as Chris Coursey at THRIVEtoday. Best of all, these skills can be practiced anywhere:

Yawning

I know this sounds too simple to work, but yawning activates the Vagus Nerve, a nerve that runs down the center of the body and connects the nervous system to the organs. When this nerve is activated by yawning, it sends a signal that tells the nervous system that all is well. [5]

Humming or Singing

Have you ever noticed that humming has a calming effect? When I feel overwhelmed by my kids, I often go to the kitchen and hum a tune while preparing a meal or washing dishes. Humming and singing are both effective in activating the Vagus Nerve and calming the nervous system as well.[6]

Entering into Grateful Memories

By taking a quiet moment and revisiting a memory that elicits gratitude, peace, and appreciation, we can calm our nervous systems and return to relational mode. I have a list of memories I revisit when I need to return to relational mode. One of my favorite memories is from a trip to our family's cabin in late autumn. I hiked to the top of a mountain and watched the sun rise over the forested hills. I felt a deep sense of peace and joy, and God's presence seemed almost tangible to me.

Most of my memories are from times when I was enjoying nature and felt especially at ease and aware of the Lord's presence with me. When I feel myself entering into fight or flight mode, I try to go somewhere quiet and enter into an appreciation memory. I recall the sights, sounds, smells, and sensations I experienced within the memory. I let the memory flood me with peace and joy and ask God to reveal himself to me within the memory. Within a few minutes, I am almost always ready to reconnect relationally with God and others.[7]

I encourage you to begin paying attention to the moments when you leave relational mode throughout your days. Use these techniques to help you calm your nervous system as you reestablish the ability to connect with God and others.

Let's now return to the country road where I'm ready to explore my emotions with the Lord.

A: Ask God Why You're Responding the Way You Are

After taking a moment to enjoy the fresh air and listen to the sound of thunder in the distance, I tell God everything I'm feeling and ask him to show me why I'm so overwhelmed.

"God, I wish I could enjoy the experience of decorating for Christmas as a family, but I'm a mess. I feel overwhelmed by the clutter, the chaos, and the fact that the kids have overtaken this process. Help me see what's beneath this stress. What's this about?" I pray.

As I walk, a thought comes to mind: *The situation—especially the mess—feels out of control.*

"Yes, Lord, that's it," I pray. "It feels out of control."

I'm tempted to be harsh with myself for my ongoing issues with releasing control. Instead, I remember the advice given to me by a friend who is also a therapist, and I approach my emotions with curiosity and compassion.

"God, help me see why it's so important for me to remain in control of the messes in my house," I pray.

Nothing comes to mind immediately. I let my mind wander and continue breathing deeply as I enjoy the fresh air. Slowly, through images, God begins to show me why I so desperately try to keep the house clean. In my mind's eye, I see myself trying to eat dinner, exercise, shower, write, cook, and even sleep. I see my children coming to me in these moments with pressing needs—interrupting my agenda—and I see myself tending to their needs.

For the first time, I identify the root of my desire for control: I cling to control over the house because motherhood has required me to release control in thousands of ways. Often, I no longer get to choose when I will eat, exercise, shower, work, cook, or sleep. I have young children, and their needs come before mine. I might think I'm about to get eight hours of sleep, but when a little boy with a tummy ache interrupts my plans, his needs come first. I might be looking forward to a hot meal or a quiet shower, but if the youngest decides he needs me, I might wait hours, or even days, to fulfill my desires.

I might not be able to take a nap or enjoy a quiet shower for days, but I can clean my floors and countertops five times a day and feel like some part of my life still belongs to me.

This revelation is startling. It is also free from condemnation and shame. I sense God's tenderness and understanding, and I know that he is inviting me to a new level of freedom.

"Father, I need you to help me release my desire for control. I cannot do this on my own," I pray. "Please help me so that this evening might be the first step toward a new way of living. Lead me to truth to stand on so that I might return to my family with a joyful, peaceful spirit."

I'll share the truth that served as an anchor for me in the next section of this chapter. First, I want to compassionately remind you that God sees your triggered moments and your meltdowns, and he's not angry with you. Instead, he is inviting you into greater freedom, peace, and maturity. Learning to ask him why you're responding in certain ways can transform your life. He wants to show you what's beneath your emotions and help you grow.

After calming down enough to connect with God relationally, he almost always shows me what's beneath my surface-level emotions. He wants to show you, too. The secret is to remember to ask him.

Now, I invite you to join me as I continue my walk, and we'll talk about our final step into grace: Standing on God's Truth.

T: Stand on Truth Instead of Standing on Your Feelings

Cold winter rain is falling from the black December sky as I ask God for truth to stand on so that I might return home with peace and joy.

With the falling rain, familiar words seem to fall from the inky darkness: "Give thanks in all circumstances." These are the words of 1 Thessalonians 5:18.

I consider what it might look like to stand on these words instead of standing on my faltering emotions. I might return to my chaotic house with gratitude for my family instead of a desire to control my environment. Perhaps I could leave the pine needles on the floor and enjoy my children's excitement. I might let the kids cover the bottom half of the tree with ornaments and laugh instead of stressing over it. Maybe I could leave the empty decoration boxes in the dining room overnight instead of frantically hurrying to return them to the basement. As the rain soaks through my jacket, the mess that seemed so overwhelming suddenly seems silly. I smile as I stride toward the house, and I sense that God is smiling on me from above.

Returning to the Chaos

Returning from my walk, I discover that more boxes of decorations have been opened. The mess has expanded. From the middle of the mess, four smiling faces greet me as they radiate Christmas joy.

After changing out of my sopping wet clothing, I join my family, and we continue sorting through the open boxes. I tell them about the decorative Santa figurines given to me by my aunt, the ornaments from my grandma, and the snowmen I once arranged as windowsill decorations in my classroom when I was a teacher. I take the time to feel each ornament and trinket and share memories as we explore each one.

Later, while the kids take baths, I pick up the pine branches scattered across the floor, but I resist the urge to sweep up every tiny pine needle. Obediently, I leave the empty decoration boxes in the dining room and go to the kitchen to prepare popcorn. I'm ready for snuggles and snacks when the little ones bound downstairs smelling like watermelon shampoo. We finish the night by turning out the lights and listening to Christmas music as we admire the colorful glow of our half-decorated tree.

The house is a mess, but my heart is filled with peace and joy—evidence that I'm moving ever closer to the life I long to live.

Your loving heavenly Father wants to help you return to peace in your triggered moments as well. The next time you're triggered, remember the CAT acrostic. Calm your nervous system, ask God for insight, and stand on truth. God is waiting to help you and transform you.

Questions for Reflection and Discussion:

1. Pause to review the past few days. Ask the Lord to remind you of a moment that sent you into fight or flight mode. How did you respond?

2. Imagine responding to the moment you just identified by walking through the three CAT steps. In what way would your response be different if you intentionally calmed your nervous system, asked God about your emotions, and stood on the truth?

3. How do you typically respond to overwhelming emotions? What are some of the benefits of processing our emotions with God?

4. Why is it important to stand on God's truth after allowing ourselves to process our emotions?

5. Throughout the upcoming day, pay attention to the moments when you leave relational mode—when you feel agitated and unable to emotionally connect with God and with others. Come back and record the moments that sent you out of relational mode. Why is it important to recognize whether or not your relational circuits are open?

Notes:

1. Cherry, K. (2019, August 18). *How the Fight or Flight Response Works.* Verywell Mind; Verywellmind. https://www.verywellmind.com/what-is-the-fight-or-flight-response-2795194

2. *Whole-Brain Living Session 3: Remain Relational 1. Joy & Peace in Scripture.* (n.d.). https://deeperwalkinternational.org/wp-content/uploads/2020/02/Whole-Brain-Living-Session-3-Notes.pdf

3. *Whole-Brain Living Session 3: Remain Relational 1. Joy & Peace in Scripture. (n.d.). https://deeperwalkinternational.org/wp-content/uploads/2020/02/Whole-Brain-Living-Session-3-Notes.pdf*

4. *Whole-Brain Living Session 3: Remain Relational 1. Joy & Peace in Scripture. (n.d.). https://deeperwalkinternational.org/wp-content/uploads/2020/02/Whole-Brain-Living-Session-3-Notes.pdf*

5. *5 Ways To Stimulate Your Vagus Nerve.* (2022, March 10). Cleveland Clinic. https://health.clevelandclinic.org/vagus-nerve-stimulation/

6. *5 Ways To Stimulate Your Vagus Nerve.* (2022, March 10). Cleveland Clinic. https://health.clevelandclinic.org/vagus-nerve-stimulation/

7. *A Splash of Appreciation - Thriving Mamas.* (2020, June 17). https://thrivingmamas.org/2020/06/17/a-splash-of-appreciation/

9

Grace for Your Body:

Treating Your Body with Tenderness

Grace Takeaway: We lean into grace when we learn to treat our bodies with the same tenderness we would extend to our most precious loved ones.

This morning I stepped out of the shower, stood in front of the mirror, and was less than thrilled about the sight in front of me. Thankfully, I wasn't looking at an unrolled trail of toilet paper or a baby playing in the toilet water (two unfortunate events that transpired recently). Instead, as I gazed at my reflection, I was consumed by critical thoughts.

With three kids in the house, I don't spend much time analyzing my appearance. Most days, I feel successful if I manage to rub a dab of lotion into my hands and apply a thin layer of mascara. I don't have time to analyze my muscle mass or rub oil on my stretchmarks.

Today was different. I showered while Aiden napped, and my older two children were enjoying a day at their grandparents' house. It was my first quiet shower in months.

As I stood in front of the mirror, I noticed parts of my appearance that bothered me. I ran my fingers over the stretchmarks on my lower abdomen. I grabbed the skin around my belly and told myself I needed to cut back on the evening snacking.

I then moved closer to the mirror and examined my face. Dark circles under my eyes revealed my weariness after a night of interrupted sleep; my summer freckles had returned in all their glory; and two gray hairs announced their presence by sticking straight out of my scalp like eager schoolchildren raising their hands for attention.

Regrettably, I've spent most of my life embracing critical thoughts about my body. This morning was no exception.

I wonder if you can relate. I wonder if you look at your body and criticize what you see.

After discussing the topic of self-criticism with dozens of friends, I've discovered that most of us deal with body shame and negative thoughts about our bodies.

We know that God loves us just the way we are, and we've read that our bodies are temples of the Holy Spirit. Sadly, instead of helping us care for our bodies with kindness, thinking of our bodies as temples of the Holy Spirit often leads to guilt and self-condemnation. We sometimes feel ashamed of the ways we treat God's temple, but we don't know how to shift into healthier relationships with our bodies.

Some of us stand in front of mirrors and criticize our hair, our complexion, or our curves. Others cringe at the thought of swimsuit season and don't let our spouses see our bodies in the light. Many of us wince when we step onto scales and feel critical when we look at our thighs in the mirror.

It's not easy to find peace with our bodies. Cultural pressures encourage us to hide our "imperfections." As a result, we spend thousands of dollars covering our blemishes, tightening our lines, and attempting to lose weight. At times, we resent our bodies for failing to conform to the images we have in our minds.

Friends, what if we stopped embracing self-critical thoughts? What if we learned to see ourselves the way God sees us and treat ourselves in ways that honor and please God?

God wants to transform our hearts by shifting our perspective when it comes to our bodies. Throughout the past few years, he has helped me change my perspective in two ways: He has helped me *see* my body through a different lens, and he has used this new perspective to help me *treat* my body with tenderness.

Return with me to the moment in front of my bathroom mirror, and we'll talk about seeing our bodies through different lenses.

Learning to See Your Body Differently

After pulling the two gray hairs from the top of my head and applying a thin layer of mascara, I wiggle into my jeans and realize they're too tight. Critical thoughts immediately race through my mind, and I consider skipping lunch as a first step toward losing a few pounds. I'm seriously contemplating how I might quickly drop five pounds when a thought floats through my mind: *Is this what you would advise your daughter to do?*

Immediately, a memory comes to mind. I recall a moment that took place when our daughter, Bekah, was just three years old.

I had just pulled her from the bathtub and wrapped her in a towel. As I tenderly dried her beautiful little body, she made a declaration I'll never forget. "Mom, I don't like my legs," she suddenly remarked. "My legs are too chubby."

I thought my heart might explode in my chest. Where did my little girl's self-critical thought come from? How does a three-year-old decide she's too chubby?

In response to little Bekah's remark, I put both hands on her small shoulders and looked directly into her eyes. With all the love in my heart, I said, "Your legs are not chubby, my beautiful girl. They are strong and healthy and just the way God made you. Don't ever compare the way God made you to the way he made

135

someone else. He made you beautiful, brave, kind, and strong, and your legs look just right."

To this day, I don't know where little Bekah got the idea that her legs were chubby. What I do know is this: When she made that self-critical comment, I wanted nothing more than to immediately speak the truth to her and reveal God's perspective to her.

In the months after that life-changing interaction with Bekah, God reminded me of the moment often. Every time I looked at *my* body with critical thoughts, God gently reminded me that he sees me the way I see Bekah.

When God looks at me, he delights in me. He is pleased with the way he designed my body, and his heart is grieved when I compare myself to others and decide I'm lacking. I am his daughter, and he rejoices over me. Like any loving parent, he wants me to learn to see my body the way he sees it—through eyes of love and care.

Dear friend, consider the shift that might take place in your mind and heart if you learned to see yourself the way you see a precious, younger loved one. Take a moment to envision your child, grandchild, niece, or any child who is dear to you. If you aren't close to any young children, you can envision someone older; however, I find this exercise most compelling when I envision a young child I care about. In my case, I envision my children.

Now, imagine you are looking at this beloved little one's body. What would you say if she told you she was too fat, too skinny, or ugly?

Most likely, you would rush to her, hug her, and say, "No, you *are* beautiful, and you don't need to change to be beautiful and precious!" You would mean these words with every fiber of your being.

Let's stay in this space—desperately wanting our young loved ones to grasp their worth and beauty—and let's soak in this truth: God feels the same way toward us when we embrace critical thoughts about our bodies. He desperately wants to run to us, hug us, and say, "No! You are *beautiful* and *precious*! I *delight* in you! I sing over you! Don't believe the lies of the enemy!"

God *cherishes* us. He knit us together in our mothers' wombs. We are *fearfully* and *wonderfully* made. We are his beloved and precious children. His heart breaks when we embrace critical thoughts about ourselves.

Before we move on to the next part of this chapter, I invite you to sit with these truths for a while. Read this section again if you need to. Imagine the way you would feel if a dear child in your life spoke self-critical words. Imagine the desire you would feel to help this little one understand God's truth about her body. Turn to Appendix B and soak in the truths about the way God sees you.

Ask God to help you comprehend the way he feels when you embrace self-critical thoughts. His heart breaks, and he longs to renew your mind with his truth. You are beautiful, precious, and divinely created.

Casting aside self-critical thoughts might be difficult if you know you need to lose weight for medical reasons, if you have a chronic condition that impacts your appearance, or if living in this world has harmed your body in some way.

We all live in the same fallen world, and our bodies await the day when Christ redeems us and gives us new, unblemished bodies. In this sense, our bodies are not the images of perfection they will be after Christ redeems his children. However, God has called us to love and care for these imperfect bodies and see them through his eyes of love.

Learning to see ourselves through the lens of love and compassion is essential if we're going to care for our bodies as temples of the Holy Spirit. Once we learn to see ourselves the way we see our cherished loved ones, our hearts are ready to *treat* our bodies the way we treat our dearest loved ones.

Treating Our Bodies with Compassion and Care

Many of us have never been taught to treat our bodies with compassion and tenderness. Just as we stand in front of mirrors and notice our flaws, we often push our bodies to perform beyond reasonable limits or treat our bodies with contempt. We would never dream of treating our children or loved ones the way we treat ourselves.

Let's consider a few examples: We wouldn't compulsively shove junk food into our children's mouths to fill their emotional voids, but we do it to our own bodies. We wouldn't force our little ones to push through sickness like nothing's wrong or get angry when their bodies are injured. We wouldn't put off their doctor's visits because we don't have time in our schedules. We wouldn't deprive them of sleep and then expect them to function at peak performance. We wouldn't deprive them of food so that they might fit into special clothing or force them to exercise for hours to compensate for eating too much the previous day. We wouldn't dream of treating our loved ones in these ways, but most of us don't think twice about treating ourselves with this lack of care.

I've spent the majority of my life pushing my body to perform. This performance-driven grit seemed to serve me well as a teenage athlete and regularly enabled me to function on only a few hours of sleep throughout my twenties. However, the long-term effects of not caring for myself eventually caught up with me. Because I pushed my body so hard as a teenage athlete, I have several chronic orthopedic conditions. Depriving my body of sleep throughout my twenties ultimately led to severe burnout.

Over time, I have learned that caring for my body with tenderness is the pathway to becoming a woman of grace. God has also taught me that the way I treat myself will eventually be projected onto others.

A woman who is harsh and critical of herself will eventually project her critical, harsh spirit onto others. In the same sense, when we learn to be tender and loving with ourselves, we increase our capacities to be tender and loving toward others.

What might it look like to begin treating our bodies with tenderness and compassion? Think of the ways we care for the bodies of the children in our lives: We limit sugar intake for the sake of health and not for the sake of chasing an elusive body image; we take time to prepare and serve healthy, well-rounded meals; we apply lotion to chafed skin and climb into bunkbeds to rub lip gloss on cracked lips; we encourage them to go outside and move their bodies instead of sitting in front of screens; we are diligent about bedtime and create space for naps; we don't skip checkups with doctors or neglect medical needs; and we offer them delicious treats at the end of long days without any hint of guilt.

What might happen if we learned to treat ourselves with these same measures of care?

Precious friend, the God who created your body gives you permission to treat yourself with compassion today. When the Apostle Paul wrote to the Corinthian church and reminded them that their bodies were temples of the Holy Spirit, he was encouraging them to live in sexual purity.[1] However, this teaching is not exclusive to matters of sexual conduct. Our bodies are not our own. They belong to God, and God is pleased when we treat our bodies with care.

What might happen if you gave yourself permission to take a nap, take a leisurely walk through your neighborhood, or make yourself a cup of tea and watch the sun sink below the horizon? We honor God by listening to our bodies and caring for ourselves. This might include taking a few extra minutes to rub moisturizer into your skin or drinking a glass of water. It might also include the more disciplined work of caring for yourself: joining a gym, visiting the doctor for a regular checkup, and intentionally filling your home with food that will replenish you.

Treating ourselves with tenderness and care isn't about following rules or restricting ourselves. Instead, it's about listening to the cues our bodies are sending and learning to respond with grace.

God is glorified when we treat our bodies with care and compassion. More importantly, when we learn to love ourselves, our capacities for loving others will expand. God's encouragement to care for ourselves is evident throughout Scripture. In addition to Paul's writing in 1 Corinthians 6:19-20, we find this directive hidden within the often-spoken words of Jesus: "You shall love your neighbor as yourself" (Matthew 19:19).

This verse is often quoted as a reminder to be kind to one another. However, it's easy to miss the practical application: When we're not good at loving ourselves, we often have a difficult time loving other people. As I shared earlier, learning to treat ourselves with care and kindness equips us to treat others with care and kindness.

Caring for our bodies is not meant to be an end in itself. Instead, God wants us to care for ourselves so that we are healthy—mentally, emotionally, and physically—and are capable of being his vessels of love in the world.

As you ask God to help you change the way you see your body and the way you treat your body, he might ask you to change some of your habits and rhythms. Bear in mind that he will never use shame to motivate this change. God always calls us to action from a place of love. He desires wholeness, health, and freedom for you.

Allowing God to change the way we see ourselves takes time and practice, but I encourage you to keep doing the work. The Lord is waiting to renew your mind and your body as you learn to love yourself and extend his grace to yourself.

Questions for Reflection and Discussion:

1. When you stand in front of the mirror, what self-critical thoughts most often come to mind? How does your perspective change when you consider your most precious loved one and aim to love yourself in the way you love this person?

2. What advice would you give to a younger woman when it comes to caring for herself?

3. I shared my tendency to push myself hard and have high expectations of my body. In what ways have you had unrealistic expectations of your body's capabilities?

4. In what ways do you neglect your body's needs as you push through your days on autopilot? Why do you overlook these needs or push them aside? What is God showing you about these needs?

5. Ask God to show you one step you can take this week to begin caring for your body with greater tenderness and compassion. What is God showing you?

Notes:

1. 1 Corinthians 6:19-20, my translation

10

Grace for Your Destructive Habits:
Eating Your Feelings

Grace Takeaway: We lean into grace when we learn to turn to God for help in the middle of our indulgent moments. From this posture of surrender, God will renew our minds and direct us into his freedom and deliverance.

I stare out the frosted windowpane and wish I could find freedom from the behavior that's been stealing my joy for years. Last night I indulged again, and I've felt disgusted and ashamed all day today.

I shared one small victory in this battle in the introduction of this book; however, finding freedom in my relationship with food continues to be an imperfect journey. At times, I feel like I'm stuck, and I wonder if I'll ever change.

Perhaps you feel stuck in some realm of your life, too. Like me, you probably tell yourself you're going to do better. Sometimes, you succeed for a day or a week or even a month. But then life gets hard, or you feel bored or stressed or sad. To escape your emotions, you do the thing you hate. You're stuck.

Stuck in the Cycle

As I gaze out my bedroom window, I consider the events that led to yesterday's failure: It was a long day at home with three energetic kids; I was tired because the little one cried half the night; the oldest two were unable to be together for longer than 11 seconds without fighting; I found six rock-hard peanut butter and jelly sandwiches behind the bookshelf in the living room; and my husband had to work late.

When my husband called to say he'd be working late, I craved an escape. Because taking a walk or getting away from the house weren't options, I decided to escape into food. I wanted chocolate, but after throwing away the box of Easter candy in the laundry room (I told you about this small victory in the introduction), I was short on chocolate.

Low on chocolate and worn down by emotions, I moved from one cupboard to the next and shoved food into my mouth until I was uncomfortably full. At first, the escape felt like bliss. A day later, my abdomen is still groaning in the aftermath of way too much junk food.

I have this sinking feeling that I'll never change. I fear I'll be stuck in this horrible cycle of eating too much and then feeling sick and ashamed for the rest of my life.

Perhaps you're familiar with this sense of frustration and shame. I don't know what your cycle looks like. It might be an unhealthy escapist behavior like eating too much, drinking too much, drifting away into some social media feed, binge-watching your favorite TV series, compulsive shopping, exercising, or abusing prescription drugs. Maybe it's a more socially acceptable behavior like workaholism, perfectionism, or materialism.

Whatever it is, the behavior has become a method of escape and comfort, but it's also become a stronghold in your life. You can't seem to quit. You've tried to quit, but willpower has failed you. You're not sure where to turn next.

This is exactly where I am as I sit on the edge of the bed in the aftermath of yet another failure with food. I'm so tired of this cycle. I'm so tired of coming up with a new plan, willing myself to change, and failing.

As I sit in the silence, I breathe deeply and whisper a familiar phrase to myself for the ten-thousandth time: "Get it together, girl."

God's Not Telling You to Get It Together

After telling myself to get it together, my mind drifts to the moment in the laundry room not long ago—the moment when I asked Jesus for help in the middle of my chocolate binge. I'm reminded that Jesus isn't telling me to get it together; instead, he

147

is asking me to run to him in the middle of my broken, messy moments.

As I reflect on his invitation, I'm taken back to the painful and rebellious season of my early twenties—a time when I believed I needed to get it together and stop intentionally sinning before surrendering my whole life to God. In those days, my sins revolved around all the wrong men and way too many parties. I believed in God, but was living in rebellion. Drawing near to God amid my brokenness and ungodly behaviors made me feel ashamed and disgusted with myself. I imagined God was disgusted with me, too.

I was wrong.

Hear this, friend.

I had it backward. So many of us have it backward. We think we need to get it together *before* we run to God. In reality, God is calling us to run to him *in the middle* of our sin, shame, and weakness. In his love, *he* will help us change, and *he* will restore us.

Looking back, I can see how God was waiting for me with open arms throughout those messy and painful years. He wasn't telling me to get t together so that I could have a deep relationship with him; instead, he was calling me to come to him in my brokenness, and in the middle of the mess, our relationship would heal me.

Precious friend, God is calling you to come to him in the middle of your imperfect, broken life and let him do the work of healing you. Breaking free from your sin is not a prerequisite for running to Jesus. Draw near to him in the middle of your sin, and *his grace* will lead you to the freedom you've been unable to find through willpower.

Sadly, even amid my ongoing struggle with food, I have it backward. Getting it together in my strength is never the criterion for coming to God. It's really the opposite: God wants me to come to him while I'm still chewing on the chocolate and say, "Help me, Lord! I need you again." This is the first step for leaning into grace when it comes to our destructive habits, habitual sins, and stuck places.

I remind myself of these truths as Aiden cries from his crib. My quiet moment with the Lord is over.

"Lord, help me find freedom in my relationship with food," I whisper as I leave the room and return to the work of the day.

Practical Ways to Find Freedom

In the time since my moment in the bedroom—the moment I just described—the Lord began offering new insights to transform my relationship with food. I have not arrived in this area of my life, and I still hide in the laundry room and eat chocolate on occasion; however, I am moving closer to the freedom I crave. Meanwhile, the insights I'm about to share have helped me step into a healthier relationship with food.

Examine Your Motives

One of the first steps for breaking free from any habitual sin pattern is asking God to align our hearts with his heart so that we embrace what he embraces and reject what he rejects.

For decades, I didn't consistently abhor my sin of abusing food. I was stuck in a cycle of idolizing food and idolizing body image. My motives for trying to eat in healthier ways didn't align with God's motives. I didn't want to overeat because I didn't want to gain weight. All I cared about was maintaining a thin body.

Meanwhile, God has never been worried about the number on the scale; he wants me to live with a sense of freedom and joy. God wants to help me find freedom in my relationship with food because he wants me to be healthy, not because he wants me in a smaller dress size.

In the weeks following my prayer in the bedroom, God began illuminating my motives for wanting to eat in healthier ways. He also began to align my heart with his heart as I aimed to treat my body the way I would treat my children's bodies. Instead of telling myself not to eat junk food so that I could stay thin, I started to say, "I want to make healthy food choices and care for my body in the same way I care for my most precious loved ones' bodies."

By God's grace, I slowly stopped criticizing my appearance and started to see myself as God sees me. I started to ask questions such as, *Would I shove handfuls of chocolate chips into my children's mouths to help them escape their realities?*

As God renewed my mind over time, eating healthier was no longer about losing weight. It was about treating myself with care and compassion and honoring God in the process. God showed me his great love and tenderness toward me, and he aligned my heart with his love and tenderness. I was able to forgive myself when I ate too much sugar, and one cookie no longer sent me into the abyss of an all-out binge. God changed my heart in such a way that I wanted to treat my body with love and care instead of criticizing and abusing it.

Regardless of what sin or habit you grapple with, ask God to show you your motives for wanting to find freedom. Do you want to stop overeating as a means to have a healthy body and honor God with your life, or are you also chasing a number on the scale?

Do you want to change an unhealthy behavior out of a sincere desire to honor the Lord? Or is your desire to change fueled by shame, embarrassment, or a longing for control?

For most of us, our answers to these questions aren't clear-cut. We want to be healthy and God-honoring, but we're also embarrassed, disgusted, and ashamed.

Let's begin by extending grace to ourselves. Let's be where we are and not try to hide our mixed motives. However, let's not stop there. After exploring all of our motives for wanting to change, we can ask God to align our hearts with his by praying a prayer like this: "Father, I feel so many emotions surrounding this behavior. When it comes to finding freedom, help my decisions to be fueled by your love and not by shame and embarrassment."

Have you ever noticed that shame and embarrassment are poor motivators for lasting change?

You might quit smoking, drinking, looking at porn, taking pills, cutting, or overeating for a few days; however, eventually, you return to the behavior. Often, the problem is that you are motivated by shame and embarrassment instead of love.

What might it look like to be motivated by love?

Let's return to the truth we explored in the previous chapter: We will be motivated to turn away from destructive behaviors when Jesus' love for us changes our hearts. In the same way that encountering the tender love of Jesus helps us see our bodies through loving eyes, we will be compelled to turn away from our unhealthy behaviors when the love of Christ permeates our lives and changes the way we see these behaviors.

We encounter the tender and compelling love of Christ by taking the time to meditate on his Word, asking him to renew our minds, practicing treating our bodies with care, and soaking in his love. As his love permeates our souls, we shift from shame-based motivation to love-based motivation, and love-based motivation moves us toward freedom from our unhealthy habits.

Ask God to show you what steps he is calling you to take as you align yourself with his desire for you, and he will show you.

In addition to transforming our motives, God also wants to show us the lies that feed our harmful behaviors. He wants to renew our minds by helping us stand on his truth instead of believing these lies. Let's explore the importance of shifting from lies to truth.

Replace Lies with God's Truth

In addition to showing me my flawed motives for wanting to eat in healthier ways, God also began to show me the lies I was believing about food. The greatest lie told me that food was my ultimate source of comfort.

In response to this realization, I changed my inner dialogue. Instead of telling myself that food was my greatest source of comfort, I started to tell myself, *God is my ultimate source of comfort.* I meditated on Bible verses about God's comfort, such as, "As a mother comforts her child, so will I comfort you" (Isaiah 66:13, NIV).

I repeated this verse hundreds of times in the months after God revealed the ie I was believing. It took time to change the neuropathways in my brain, but I eventually began to believe that God offers greater comfort than food.

God is inviting you to uncover the lies that are feeding your destructive habits or habitual sins as well. To find these lies, it might help to ask what your flesh is telling you about the behavior. Is your flesh saying something like, "This habit is my source of comfort, escape, or release"?

Find the lie that is feeding your behavior, and then dig into your Bible and find a truth to speak when the lie tells you to indulge. Speak the verse day after day. Speak the verse when you fail (because we all fail). Ask God to renew your mind. Here are a few examples of the lies we believe and the truths that help us align our hearts and minds with the Lord:

Lie: *I indulge because I deserve a reward at the end of the day.* **Truth:** *Jesus is my great reward, my comfort, and my portion (see Revelation 22:12, John 14:27, and Psalm 73:26).*

Lie: *My husband doesn't meet my needs, so I have to meet them somewhere.* **Truth:** *No good thing will God withhold from those who walk blamelessly (see Psalm 84:11).*

Lie: *I can't say no, and I am powerless.* **Truth:** *God will not allow you to be tempted beyond what you can bear, and he will always provide a way out of your temptation (see 1 Corinthians 10:13).*

Lie: *It's worth indulging because when I indulge, my worries and cares disappear.* **Truth:** *Cast your cares on him, and he will sustain you (see Psalm 55:22).*

Lie: *It doesn't hurt anyone, and I like the way it makes me feel.* **Truth:** *Everything is permissible, but not everything is beneficial (see 1 Corinthians 10:23).*

Your habit is most likely causing damage to your body, mind, emotions, or spirit. You might feel ashamed, disgusted, corrupted, or physically ill as a result of your habit. Most likely, self-effort has been telling you to get it together and stop being such a failure. When you mess up, self-effort condemns you and tells you you'll never find freedom. Self-effort tells you to try harder, buckle down, and punish yourself for your failures.

Your self-effort has good intentions. Thank your self-effort for these intentions. Then, ask self-effort to step aside as you lean into God's grace. Remind yourself that God looks at you in the same way you look at your most precious loved one. His thoughts toward you are tender, kind, and full of compassion. As you walk toward freedom, continue to ask God to help you treat yourself with tender care. Shame and condemnation will not lead you to freedom.

Refuse to give in to shame and condemnation when you fail. Instead, imagine Jesus taking hold of your hand, helping you to your feet, and encouraging you to continue walking forward. He is leading you toward the freedom you long for.

Set Grace-Based Boundaries

In addition to replacing lies with God's truth, asking God to help us establish grace-based boundaries will help us step into the freedom awaiting us. As I shared earlier, it's important to remember that God calls us to set boundaries for our good, not to take away our fun.

Sometimes, we need to draw hard lines and turn away from certain habits permanently. For example, there's no room for even a hint of sexual impurity in our lives. For those who battle with addiction to controlled substances, walking away from the substance is the only option.

With other habits—such as my struggle with food—extreme deprivation might be detrimental. I'm an all-or-nothing kind of girl, and I've realized that excessive restriction leads me to a mindset that could easily result in an eating disorder. For this reason, I avoid a deprivation mindset as much as possible.

The key to setting boundaries is to seek the Lord in prayer and seek wise counsel from others. Through wise counsel, prayer, and the direction given in the Bible, God wants to lead us to set appropriate boundaries that will work for us.

You might need to change your routines, change the food and beverage choices in your home, throw a few things away, find healthy replacement activities, set boundaries around your online shopping habits, or create space for healthy forms of self-care within your day. Follow wherever you sense the Lord is leading and remember this: God's boundaries are for your good.

My grace-based boundaries involving food include a loose schedule of balanced eating every three to five hours. I eat similar meals at similar times of the day every day of the week because I thrive on patterns and consistent habits. My eating habits probably wouldn't work for most people, but these boundaries work for me.

Ask God to show you what sorts of boundaries will help set you up for success. It will probably take trial and error, but your loving heavenly Father wants to lead you to freedom and joy. He will show you the way.

"Keep It Real" with Someone You Trust

Lastly, bringing our destructive behavior patterns into the light with others helps us find freedom. God designed us to live in community with others. The encouragement and accountability we find with other believers are vital for many reasons.

When we share our struggles with others, we discover that we're not the only ones battling sin. Shame is dispelled when we realize that we're not alone.

I've been leading small groups of women for decades, and the most powerful conversations are often the ones in which we all open up about our most shameful sins. Women have found a safe place in my home to talk about self-injury, prescription drug abuse, exercise addiction, eating disorders, alcohol abuse, and the temptation to look at porn (This is a common struggle for both men and women, and you are not alone if you battle this temptation, friend!).

We heal in community.

Chains break in community.

God uses other people to encourage us when we fail and provide strength when we feel weak.

My friend Beth often thanks me for "keeping it real" with her. In other words, I tell her how I'm *actually* doing, regularly confess my sins to her, and tell her if I'm feeling tempted to indulge in sin. I have a few close friends with whom I always keep it real. I know I can send a text message to these friends any hour—day or night—and simply say, "I'm struggling with temptation. Please pray."

These friends will pray, and they will also check in with me to see how I'm doing. They are gentle with my failures, but they also encourage me to keep pursuing God and walking with him.

If you don't have any of these people in your life, ask God to give you just one or two friends with whom you can keep it real. Keeping it real with others is a game-changer.

After you reflect on your habits using the questions below, we'll take a journey into the tender love of Christ in Chapter Eleven. This love has the power to overcome any sin, and I pray you will find more tools to help you walk in freedom.

Questions for Reflection and Discussion:

1. What unhealthy habit would you like to overcome? Describe your journey with this habit.

2. What is your primary motivation for wanting to change this behavior? It might help to fill in the blank in the following statement: "If I can quit this behavior, then_____."

3. Is walking in God's freedom and joy your only motivation for wanting to change, or is there shame and embarrassment involved? What is God showing you about *his* motivating desire for you to change?

4. What lie feeds your unhealthy behavior? What truth from Scripture can you speak when this lie comes to mind and tempts you to indulge?

5. What boundaries can you set to help set yourself up for future success with this behavior? Ask God to guide you.

11

Grace for Your Relationship with Jesus: Experiencing the Tender Love of Christ

Grace Takeaway: We lean into grace when we create space for the tender love of Christ to capture our hearts.

Today, I invite you to imagine we're sitting on my couch together with mugs of our favorite steaming beverages in our hands. We're wearing our comfiest sweatpants and feeling safe to be completely real with one another. There's a plate of blueberry muffins on the dining room table, and my coconut-scented candle flickers on the end table.

In this safe space, I ask, "Are the ways you're seeking Jesus leading you into life-giving encounters with him?"

I hope you grab my hands and say, "Yes! Let me tell you about what he's showing me!"

If this is your response, I'm all ears, and I'm about to ask you everything you're doing so that I can follow your lead.

However, you might look at me with an uncertain expression on your face and say, "Sometimes," or you might look into your steaming mug and say, "I'm not sure I even know what it means to encounter Jesus in a life-giving way."

Regardless of how you imagine yourself responding to my question, I want to look into your eyes right now and tell you that it's normal for your relationship with the Lord to experience hills, valleys, plateaus, and even deserts. The secret to growing with Jesus is realizing that when we feel disconnected from him, we may need to pursue him in different ways in order to go deeper with him.

Jesus is always calling us to go deeper. We will spend eternity receiving deeper and deeper revelations of Christ's love for us, and we will never reach the bottom of his love or fully grasp his tenderness toward us. Today, we're going to stay in the safe space—the space where we're two friends sharing our hearts over coffee, green tea, or whatever you like to drink—and we're going to explore what it might look like for you to have a life-changing encounter with the tenderness of Jesus Christ.

I have strategically placed this chapter following the chapters about being tender with our bodies and turning to Jesus in the middle of our sinful moments because experiencing Christ's love in deeper, life-giving ways positions us to walk in freedom in these areas. The purpose of this chapter is to help you learn how to experience the tenderness of Jesus and let that tenderness transform your life.

We're going to explore what it might look like for you to go deeper with Jesus, and I'll share two principles that have helped me develop deeper relational intimacy with the Lover of my Soul: Committing to a daily sacred time with Jesus and experiencing Jesus using sanctified imagination. Let's jump in and continue our conversation as if we're sitting in my living room together.

Daily Commitment to Spending Time with Jesus

Throughout the previous chapters, I've mentioned that I often begin my days by sitting beside the window with Jesus. Almost every morning, I gather my Bible, journal, a bowl of dry cereal, and a cup of coffee, and I go to the window to soak in Jesus' love.

I'll be the first to admit that there are days when distractions and to-do lists pull me away from the window. When furry bunnies are hopping through my house, children are beckoning me, and Wonder Woman Syndrome is calling, I've been known to miss my time with the Lord. However, missing my time with Jesus always leaves my spirit feeling the same way my body feels when deprived of food—I feel undernourished. On the days when I miss my time with Jesus, I feel scattered, uncentered, and empty throughout the entire day.

Pause with me, friend, and imagine that as we're sitting on my couch, I tenderly put my hand on your forearm and say, "I know it's hard to find time to meet with Jesus when life is full. I know it's hard with noisy kids, a job that starts at the crack of dawn, or a thousand other commitments fighting for your time and attention. I know it's hard because it's hard for me, too. But I've also realized that deciding to make this time a top priority has radically shaped my spiritual life. When might you be able to make this work?"

I encourage you to pause right now, take a serious look at the rhythms of your days, and ask God to show you when you might regularly find a few quiet moments with him.

After we commit to setting aside a certain time for meeting with Jesus, it's helpful to identify a specific space where we can draw near to him. I sit by the window because I've always felt closest to God in nature. Looking outside also pulls my attention away from the messes in my house and away from the noise my kids are making. I even use a white noise generator on my phone to drown out the sounds coming from different parts of the house.

Once we've set aside a time and a space, we can begin thinking about the methods we will use for connecting with the Lord. My time at the window almost always includes several disciplines that help me connect with the loving presence of Jesus: I cultivate gratitude, confess my sins, soak in Jesus' presence, and pursue the Word.

The order in which I practice these disciplines varies, but my time with Jesus is most life-giving when I incorporate each of them at some point during my quiet time. Join me by the window, and I'll tell you more.

Cultivate Gratitude

I often begin my time with Jesus by thanking him for the gifts in my life. For years, I always started by thanking him for three gifts from the previous day. When that was no longer refreshing, I began thanking him for just one gift and spending a few minutes savoring everything I appreciated about that one gift (as I described earlier in this book).

In a different season, I gave thanks for five specific blessings each morning: I thanked Jesus for a person, an event from the previous day, something beautiful, something difficult, and an attribute of God. I named these five gifts by listing them in a journal.

Regardless of the method for giving thanks, gratitude is important because of the work it does in our brains. As I shared earlier, appreciation activates circuits in our brains that enable us to connect with others relationally, and this includes connecting with Jesus.[1] By giving thanks, we are preparing our neural networks to connect with the Lord. We are also aligning ourselves with God's exhortation to pray with thankful hearts.

Confess Sins

After giving thanks, I usually move to a time of confession. I ask the Lord to search my heart and show me the times when I sinned against him throughout the past day. Confessing my sins every day is powerful because the Lord uses this time to show me the parts of my life that aren't bringing him glory. When I confess these sins and ask God for wisdom, he shows me practical ways to change.

God often brings to mind a misspoken word, attitude, or action. I confess the sin to him, receive his forgiveness, and ask him to empower me to walk in obedience. Sometimes, I feel prompted by the Holy Spirit to reach out to my closest friends and confess my sins. This is particularly powerful if it's a behavior I've been repeating or if I feel especially burdened by it.

Not long ago, God showed me that I had been especially impatient with my son throughout the previous day. I'd snapped at him multiple times and had been unkind. I confessed this behavior to God and asked him to help me be more loving and patient. I then texted a friend and shared my struggle with her. My friend encouraged me to apologize to my son. Taking her advice, I went to the living room, sat down beside him on the couch, and sincerely apologized. The Lord used the situation to change my heart. Since that day, when I feel tempted to snap at my little boy, I remember my commitment to be loving and patient.

Soak in Jesus' Presence

After giving thanks and confessing my sins, my soul is ready to soak in Jesus' presence. Gratitude has done the work of preparing my neural networks to commune with him, and I feel cleansed after confessing my sins and receiving his forgiveness. It's time to rest in his love.

Soaking in Jesus' presence can take many forms. Sometimes, I gaze out the window, admire the formations of the clouds, and rest in Jesus' love. Other times, I listen to worship music that stirs my heart. Often, I imagine Jesus holding me in his arms, and I relax in the comfort of his love. I remind myself of how much he enjoys me, and I bask in his delight. I also use this time to meet with Jesus through the realm of sanctified imagination. I'll share more about this later in the chapter.

Soaking is all about creating space to rest in Jesus' love. It's a gesture that reminds me that he loves to spend time with me and delights in me.

Pursue the Word

Lastly, Scripture is the primary tool God uses to renew our minds, and it's important to nourish ourselves with God's Word daily.

Right now, I'm reading through the Bible using a daily one-year reading plan. In the past, I have read according to one-year chronological Bibles and various guides compiled by different authors.

My methods of interacting with Scripture vary. Sometimes, I read the daily reading and ask God to lead me to a verse that speaks to my heart. I write the verse in my journal and reflect on it by writing about it. Other times, I read until I sense God speaking to me, which might mean reading anywhere from one verse to many chapters. I then reflect on the verse that speaks to my heart by writing about it in a journal, meditating on it, or talking to God about it. I also enjoy imagining I'm an eyewitness within the context of the Bible story I'm reading.

During this time, I often write verses on notecards and commit them to memory, read commentaries, and cross-reference verses using websites like Biblehub.com and Biblegateway.com.

When I realize that the way I'm interacting with my Bible isn't helping me connect with the Lord, I ask God to show me what I need to change. I often feel inspired to try a new reading plan, journal in a different way, or search for a new approach to help me interact with the Word differently.

When it comes to spending time with the Lord, I'd like to note that although I have a basic structure for my time with him, I try to remain open to letting him direct our time. The structure helps me to move into a mental, emotional, and spiritual space where I've created room for the Holy Spirit to move and guide me. In this way, my quiet time with the Lord is not merely an act of going through the motions; it becomes a time for engaging with the Living God.

For example, if I'm especially moved while worshiping in song, I might use most of my time worshiping. If the first Bible verse I read leaps off the page like it was written directly for me, I might spend the entire time writing about the verse, studying it, or writing about how it applies to my life. Some days, I spend most of my time writing in my prayer journal as I process difficult situations with God.

It's also important to remember that this sacred time with God is not about checking the "Quiet Time" boxes off of our daily to-do lists. We set aside this time because we want to encounter Jesus.

Encountering Jesus will always transform our lives. This truth leads me to the second principle that has helped me experience the tenderness of the Lord like nothing else: encountering Jesus through my sanctified imagination.

Sanctified Imagination

I'm not sure who coined the term "sanctified imagination," but this practice refers to the process of asking the Lord to fill every part of our minds with his Spirit and meet with us within the realm of our imaginations. Sanctification is the process of setting something apart for holy use. When we ask the Holy Spirit to sanctify our imaginations, we are asking him to use this part of our minds for his design and purpose.

Jesus told us to love the Lord our God with all our hearts, souls, *minds*, and strength, and imagination falls into the realm of loving God with all of our minds.

Before we discuss this principle, it's important to note that there is room for error when using our imaginations. We should always test our experiences in this area against the authority of Scripture, and it's also helpful to share our experiences with trusted believers. With this in mind, we don't need to be afraid of our imaginations.

You might feel skeptical about using this part of your mind for connecting with Jesus, but this skepticism is often the enemy's tactic to keep us from experiencing life-changing encounters with the Lord. When Jesus walked on the earth, he frequently relied on the human imagination when expressing spiritual truths. All of the parables included imaginative scenarios in which biblical principles were revealed.

With this in mind, let's consider the ways you might have used your sanctified imagination without realizing it: imagining the Triune God seated on his heavenly throne, imagining Jesus holding you during a difficult time, envisioning how it must have felt to behold Jesus' death on the cross, or imagining what it might have felt like to be present when Jesus performed the miracles described in the Gospels. These moments are often some of the most impactful moments in our faith.

Now, let's talk about how we might invite Jesus to minister to us through this part of our minds.

One of my favorite ways to connect with Jesus through sanctified imagination is to read the description of heaven's throne room in Revelation 4. I read slowly and imagine I'm standing before the throne, surrounded by the heavenly host, gazing at the crystal sea of glass as lightning flashes around me. I come before the Lord in worship, and I simply imagine him as he sits on his throne. Sometimes, nothing surprising happens; nevertheless, the worshipful moment fills my heart with joy. Other times, I sense the Lord inviting me to release something I've been holding onto, revealing truth to me, or offering insight into my life.

Another use of sanctified imagination is imagining myself as an onlooker or participant in a Bible story as I briefly mentioned earlier in the chapter. For example, I have imagined myself as the blind beggar along the road (Matthew 10:46-52), one of the women at Jesus' tomb (John 20:11-18), the paralytic lowered through the roof (Matthew 9:1-8), and angry Martha stomping around the kitchen (Luke 10:38-42). By entering into these narratives, the Lord often shines new light on his Word and helps me apply it to my life in fresh ways.

At the end of stressful days, I often connect with Jesus by imagining I'm resting in a beautiful and peaceful place (usually somewhere in nature). I let all five of my senses engage in the scene surrounding me, and then I invite Jesus to come and show me what he wants me to know. Most of the time, I imagine him sitting with me, and his presence fills me with peace. Other times, he enters the scene and offers insight, encouragement, comfort, or hope.

Jesus can also bring healing to traumatic memories through our imaginations. What I'm going to share with you throughout the remainder of this chapter is difficult for me to write about because it is very close to my heart. It feels raw and vulnerable, and I have fears about being misunderstood. However, after much prayer, I feel led to share these experiences with you because I want to help you discover the healing power of Christ, too. I sincerely thank you for holding my vulnerability with grace.

My first experience with sanctified imagination took place before I had a phrase to describe it. At the time, I didn't even know whether my experience was biblical; I knew only that Jesus' presence healed me.

I was in my early thirties, and for several months, I'd been having vivid visual flashbacks of the most shameful sins of my late teens and early twenties. One evening, I attended a worship service at our church, and the presence of God was palpable in the room. I sensed Jesus inviting me to sit down and let the flashbacks come.

One at a time, as each of the three shameful flashbacks came to mind, Jesus showed me his presence within the flashback. In one scenario, he was knocking on a closed door like a loving Father who had come to rescue me. In another, he took my hand and lovingly helped me walk away from the situation. In the most painful flashback, he walked into the room, scooped me into his arms, carried me outside, and told me that he would always come for me when I cried out to him.

Recognizing Jesus' presence with me healed me from the trauma of my flashbacks, and I've never struggled with the flashbacks since that day.

A few years later, after our second child, Caleb, was born, I wrestled with the traumatic memory of his birth for months. Caleb's birth was a planned C-section, and the anesthesia did not take full effect. As a result, I experienced excruciating burning and unbearable abdominal pain during the surgery. I also vomited throughout the entire process. Needless to say, it wasn't a fantastic memory.

I wanted to delight in the day our son entered into the world instead of shutting down when it came to mind. I also knew that I needed to heal from the trauma before we tried to get pregnant again. After dealing with the traumatic memory for a few months, I felt led to revisit the memory and ask Jesus to let me see his presence in the room.

I expected to see Jesus standing at the foot of the bed or standing beside me while holding my hand. Instead, the vision that came to mind wrecked me as I experienced his tenderness like never before: I was strapped cruciform to the operating table for the C-section delivery. When I asked Jesus to help me see him, he was crouched down to my left with his cheek against mine and both of his arms spread over mine in love and protection. He whispered, "I lay cruciform so that you might have life. Thank you for lying cruciform so that your child might have life."

I couldn't have made that up in my wildest dreams. Experiencing Jesus' presence within the difficult memory healed the trauma, and I never again felt paralyzed with emotional pain when I recalled the day of Caleb's birth.

My heart overflows with the tenderness of Jesus as I share these experiences with you. His love has forever captured my heart. He wants to capture your heart, too. He wants to reveal himself to you like never before.

Perhaps you have experienced a traumatic moment, and you deal with difficult memories. Maybe you have flashbacks to a sinful moment that elicits deep shame. I encourage you to find some time in the next few days to go to a quiet place and ask Jesus to let you see his presence in your memory. Test your experience against what you know about Jesus' character as revealed in Scripture, and consider sharing it with another believer, but do not be afraid. Jesus is waiting.

I also want to note that sometimes, when I ask Jesus to show me his presence in a difficult memory, I don't sense his presence. If this happens to you, don't be discouraged. Jesus is always with us, but there are times when our spiritual eyes have trouble seeing him. If you don't see or sense Jesus in your memory, rest assured that he was with you, and he was loving you.

Possibly, you don't have any unresolved traumatic memories, but you have never sensed Jesus' tenderness toward you. I encourage you to go to a quiet place, close your eyes, and imagine you are somewhere peaceful and beautiful—perhaps a beach you once visited or a peaceful scene within your imagination. After you feel relaxed, invite Jesus to join you and ask him to reveal his tenderness to you. This experience can lead you deeper into the reservoir of his love for you.

Jesus' Presence When Life Turns Upside Down

Before we close this chapter, I want you to imagine we're still sitting on my couch together. I've just shared the story about Caleb's birth and Jesus' presence in the room. You can tell by my body language that sharing this very personal story makes me feel vulnerable and even a bit awkward. However, you sense that I'm sharing it with you because I want you to experience Jesus as I have experienced him. Now, imagine I warmly look into your eyes as I ask this hard question, "Have you ever felt like Jesus abandoned you at a difficult time?"

Maybe your story didn't end with a healthy baby going home in your arms. Perhaps your loved one died, or you're still waiting for your miracle. You might feel angry because you prayed for Jesus to intervene, but as far as you can tell, he didn't. Your heart is broken.

Dear friend, I don't have answers for why some of our stories end in tears of joy, and others end in grief. I wish I could hug you and cry with you and talk through the tough questions with you. Ultimately, all I know is this: God's ways are not our ways, but we can trust him. His love for us is relentless, and he proved it when he allowed his Son to take our punishment and die on the cross for us.

When we weep, Jesus weeps with us, and he will one day restore our broken hearts. Until then, keep pursuing him. You will seek him and find him when you seek him with your whole heart.

Questions for Reflection and Discussion:

1. At the beginning of the chapter, we imagined sitting on my couch together, and I asked you if the ways you're pursuing Jesus are currently leading you into life-giving encounters with him. How did you answer my question?

2. Do you have a designated time and place where you meet with Jesus regularly? Share your experience with designating daily time with Jesus. Has this worked for you? Why or why not?

3. As you reflect on your days, when might you find time for connecting with Jesus daily? What makes this difficult for you in your current season?

4. I shared the four disciplines I use within my daily time with Jesus: cultivating gratitude, confessing sins, soaking in Jesus' presence, and pursuing the Word. Which of these disciplines could you add to your daily quiet time to help you encounter Jesus during this time?

5. Have you ever encountered Jesus through your sanctified imagination? If so, what did he reveal to you? Do you feel any resistance toward connecting with Jesus in this way? What do you fear?

6. What emotions stirred in your heart as you read about my encounters with Jesus and the way he healed some of my past trauma through sanctified imagination? Do you sense a longing for him? How will you respond?

Notes:

1. Wilder, J., & Willard, D. (2020). *Renovated : God, Dallas Willard & the church that transforms*. Navpress.

12

Grace for Insecurities:

Looking Outward Instead of Inward

Grace Takeaway: We lean into grace when we learn to focus outward instead of inward.

Our previous three chapters have led us into some deep conversations. Before we move in a different direction, I invite you to spend as much time as you need to with the previous chapters. Consider them sources of truth to which you can return as you draw near to God and lean into his grace. Continue to create space to seek him regarding the way you see your body, your besetting sins, and your relationship with Jesus.

When you feel ready to talk about insecurities, we'll have a lighthearted conversation about my lack of rhythm on the dance floor.

I begin this chapter with a scenario I have experienced multiple times: attending a wedding without a date.

If you've ever shared this experience, you know it can be intimidating. First, you have to figure out where to sit for the ceremony, and you'll likely end up sitting next to the bride's elderly great-aunt and making small talk about the decorations.

179

The reception is even more awkward, and you'll probably find yourself next to an empty chair at a circular table meant to accommodate couples. You'll peruse the dessert table when it's time for slow dancing, and if you're like me, you'll consider how to casually slip out the door when "The Electric Slide" starts blaring through the speakers.

This is all fresh in my mind after attending a friend's wedding. My parents weren't available to watch the kids, so my supportive husband agreed to stay home with the crew while I attended the wedding alone. In theory, it sounded like a good idea. It seemed like far less of a good idea as I scanned the seats and tried to figure out where to sit for the ceremony.

Approaching the rows of happy attendees, I searched the crowd for a familiar face. I spotted a few, but there were no available seats near the people I knew. Familiar thoughts raced through my mind: *Will I be included, or will I feel awkward all evening? Who will help me feel like I belong here? Was attending this wedding by myself a huge mistake?*

I immediately caught myself. I thought of Emily P. Freeman's words in her book *The Next Right Thing*:

> When I'm hanging on to the false narrative of my own life, I walk into the room thinking, "Here I am, so what are they thinking of me?" rather than, "There you are, welcome." I

walk in lonely, looking for approval, rather than in solitude with Jesus, looking to build a connection with others. We bring what we believe about ourselves and what we believe about God into every situation, gathering, and decision. . . . I want to walk into rooms with presence and on purpose, aware of people for God's sake rather than for my sake. I want to pay attention to how all the rooms in my life may poke and prod at my desire to be relevant, spectacular, and powerful.[1]

Emily's words reminded me of my reason for attending the wedding in the first place. I was there to love and support my friend. I told myself I wasn't there to be relevant, spectacular, or powerful. I wasn't there to fit in. I was there because God had called me to show up for my friend.

With these thoughts in mind, I slipped into a single seat beside a lovely young woman who once attended a Bible study at my house. We talked about our kids and enjoyed catching up until the bridal procession began. I breathed a sigh of relief. I'd survived the first round of wedding awkwardness.

An hour later, I reminded myself of Emily P. Freeman's words again as I walked into the reception and realized there were no assigned seats. I was on my own.

"Lord, who are you calling me to include, love, and connect with?" I quietly prayed, reminding the 14-year-old within me that I wasn't there to fit in.

Much to my surprise, the girls in the bridal party flagged me to their table. They were all members of a small group I led when they were in high school a decade earlier. Encouraging me to take a seat at the "head table," I looked around and humbly accepted, feeling honored they would want me to join them.

We talked about life, recounted hilarious memories of their crazy high school antics, and shared lots of laughs over dinner. Because I was at the head table, I was also seated with the bride's immediate family.

"Are you going to dance?" the mother of the bride asked me as we sipped our water.

"I wasn't planning on it," I laughed. "Dancing with my husband at a wedding is one thing. Hitting the dance floor by myself is different."

As the words left my mouth, I immediately recalled a conversation with my friend (the bride) a few years earlier. She talked about attending a wedding and dancing even though she didn't want to because she knew it would make the bride feel loved.

I reflected on the gift I might give to *my* friend by dancing awkwardly at *her* wedding, and I knew what God was calling me to do. He was calling me to dance.

Twenty minutes later, I found myself where I never expected to be—surrounded by 26-year-olds (and two fellow 40-somethings who were equally committed to making the bride feel loved)—dancing the night away.

It was hilarious.

It was awkward.

I only knew the words to songs that were at least 15 years old.

But I danced anyway.

I danced, and I didn't worry about what people were thinking because I knew my friend would be happy that I was celebrating her day with her. I took my eyes off of myself and looked for a need, and that need was supporting my friend despite my lack of rhythm.

Do you know what else happened?

I had a blast.

I had much more fun than I would have had sitting self-consciously at my table wondering if I looked pretty in my dress. I was part of a tiny group of women who hit the dance floor with no rhythm, not a single drop of alcohol flowing through our bodies, and no recognition of the music being played. Nonetheless, we danced. The joy we experienced was palpable, and it only happened because I stopped looking inward at my insecurities. I stopped wondering what others were thinking about me and, instead, asked God how to meet the needs surrounding me.

The Power of Looking Outward

Most of us know all about looking inward and dwelling on our insecurities. We walk into crowded rooms and wonder what other people are thinking about us. Some of us don't want to be noticed; we're content to slip into the crowd as inconspicuously as possible, and our primary goal is to fit in and find a place to belong. Others love to be noticed—walking into crowded rooms and wanting to be the life of every party.

Whether we try to fit in or aim to stand out, we're falling into the same trap: the trap of looking inward. It's the trap of fixing our eyes on ourselves and focusing on making an impression. And do you know what happens when we focus inward? We miss the God-given assignments surrounding us. We also miss out on the joy that comes from living a life that's not all about us.

It seems like a paradox, but the pathway to greater joy is found through giving our lives away. Jesus offers these words about giving our lives away: "The one who has found his life will lose it, and the one who has lost his life on My account will find it" (Matthew 10:39).

Most of us know we should focus less on ourselves and more on others, but this is not the natural inclination of the flesh. The flesh is always looking inward—often striving to fit in. Meanwhile, as a work of grace, God wants to set us free from self-focus and teach us to live with our eyes focused outward, always watching for the needs surrounding us.

I got it right at the wedding, but I don't always get it right. I catch myself walking into crowded rooms and feeling insecure and awkward—wondering who will make me feel included or worrying about what others think of me. Most likely, in some areas of your life, you've been a little too concerned with the opinions of others. You might have started a new job and put excessive effort into making sure you looked perfect and fit in with your coworkers. Maybe you joined a new Bible study and showed up every week wondering what the other women thought about your wardrobe, your hair, or your knowledge of the book of Obadiah.

At some point in our lives, most of us will face the temptation to compensate for our insecurities by proving how hard-working, godly, pretty, patient, creative, or loving we are. Unfortunately, when we're trying to prove something, our gaze is focused in the wrong direction.

Taking our eyes off of ourselves and living with an outward focus doesn't come naturally to most of us. If we rely on self-effort to shift our focus, we will most likely be disappointed by the inability to change ourselves. We need God to align our hearts with his heart as he does within us something we can't do for ourselves.

Today, we'll talk about two ways to lean into grace and allow God to shift our gaze from inward insecurities to the outward needs surrounding us: renewing our minds with God's Word and letting people see our authentic selves.

Renewing Our Minds with God's Word

By now, you're probably noticing a pattern throughout the pages of this book: Asking God to renew our minds with his Word is a fundamental step for leaning into his grace in every area of our lives. God's Word is powerful, and it is the primary tool he uses to renew our minds.

When it comes to fixing our attention outward on others instead of inward on ourselves, Scripture has a lot to say. While the world urges us to obsess over ourselves and what other people think about us, Scripture calls us to lose sight of ourselves in the pursuit of putting other people first. Here are a few examples:

"For whoever wants to save his life will lose it, but whoever loses his life for My sake and the gospel's will save it" (Mark 8:35).

"Do nothing from selfish or empty conceit, but with humility consider one another as more important than yourselves" (Philippians 2:3).

"Greater love has no one than this, that a person will lay down his life for his friends" (John 15:13).

"Submit to one another out of reverence for Christ" (Ephesians 5:21, NIV).

Throughout the past decade, I've memorized dozens of Bible verses about putting others first. I need to renew my mind again and again because my natural inclination is to return to self-focus. The more I allow God's Word to wash over me, the more these words change the way I see myself and the way I see the world around me.

The more we learn to live with an outward focus, the more fruit we will bear. We will become the kind of people who are known for our love, joy, peace, patience, kindness, and goodness.

We will be the kind of people who know how to create safe spaces for others to show up and be real as well.

Think about it, do you feel safe to be authentic when you're feeling insecure and trying to fit in with a group of people? I sure don't.

I invite you to travel with me to a Christian women's conference I attended a few years ago as I offer an example of what it might look like to let God renew our minds in moments of insecurity.

I've been to plenty of women's conferences, but this one was different. This conference required an eight-hour drive and included three nights spent in an elegant hotel. Attending the conference meant leaving my family for a full weekend (something I had never done), investing a large amount of money, and taking a giant leap of faith.

I went to the conference because I felt called by God to attend. It was an opportunity to learn more about following the Lord's calling as a Christian writer, and I was eager to learn and grow.

I arrived at the hotel on a humid summer evening and immediately felt about a million miles out of my comfort zone. The decorations were too fancy; the other women were too pretty; and I felt sporty, frumpy, and entirely out of place.

I spent the first day of the conference trying to fit in among the beautiful women with their perfect hair and trendy outfits—striving to portray the pretty and poised version of myself. Crashing onto my bed in exhaustion at the end of the first long day, I asked God what he wanted me to know about the day. A verse immediately came to mind: "Those who refresh others will themselves be refreshed" (Proverbs 11:25, NLT). I knew God was asking me to change my perspective as I prepared for the next day. He was calling me to take my eyes off of myself and, instead, look for women who needed his love.

The second day of the conference was remarkably different than the first—in a beautiful way. I stopped worrying about my clothes and the crazy thing the humidity was doing to my hair. I walked into that conference room as the authentic version of myself, set aside every facade, and looked for women who needed God's love.

I was honest about my life and shared my weaknesses when we sat together in discussion groups. I laughed often and deeply. God led me to several women who were desperate for his love and encouragement, and I quickly realized that God's purposes for the weekend extended far beyond learning more about writing.

I *did* glean valuable insights about crafting books and writing relatable blog posts, but I also walked away from the weekend carrying a valuable lesson. God used the conference to teach me that no matter where I go, my calling is to resist the urge to focus on myself, and, instead, look for other people who need his love. This leads us to the second way we lean into grace and let God shift our focus: letting people see our true selves.

Letting People See the Real You

Shortly after the women's conference, our family was invited to a picnic at the home of an acquaintance. Before we loaded the family into the car that afternoon, I reminded myself that I wouldn't know many of the families at the event and asked God to lead me to someone to love and encourage.

After arriving at the picnic, I noticed a woman sitting alone at a table. After casually sitting down beside her, we talked about the weather and our kids and all the normal things moms like to chat about. Somehow, the conversation turned to the stress we feel in the checkout aisle of the local discount grocery store. We shared stories of dropping glass jars of salsa on the floor, cringing beneath the irritated glare of the least-friendly cashier, and awkwardly bagging our groceries outside in snowstorms just to escape the stress inside the store. We both laughed until we cried.

We didn't unpack any major theological truths, and I didn't tell my new friend about my relationship with Jesus, but I'm sure

Jesus was pleased with our time together. It was real. There were no facades, and our time was threaded with joy.

I walked away from that picnic with a full heart and a new friend. The evening was fruitful because God helped me take my eyes off my insecurities and look for someone to love.

Like any other habit, learning to look outward instead of inward takes practice. Let's spend a few minutes reflecting on Jesus' words, and then we'll consider what it might look like to shift to an outward focus in the insecure realms of our lives.

Jesus calls us to find our lives by losing them for his sake. Here are his words: "The one who has found his life will lose it, and the one who has lost his life on My account will find it" (Matthew 10:39).

Take a quiet moment to reflect on these words. Ask God what it would look like to lose your life for his sake today. Imagine the situations you will face, the people you will interact with, and the moments when you will feel tempted to focus on your insecurities. What might it look like to shift from inward thinking to outward thinking?

Instead of asking ourselves, "What do these people think about me?" let's practice asking, "How can I love and encourage someone else in this situation?"

As you practice looking outward instead of looking inward, you will discover the most remarkable shift: God will work in your heart to help you rise above even your greatest insecurities. Instead of using your energy to focus on yourself, you'll find the freedom to watch for the needs surrounding you and carry the love of Christ to those who need it.

Questions for Reflection and Discussion:

1. How do you typically respond when you feel awkward in a group of people? What is God showing you about this response?

2. It's not wrong to want to fit in. However, we shouldn't let this desire dictate our behavior and distract us from God's calling to love others. When we're more concerned with image management than loving others, we miss out on the joy that comes from joining God's kingdom work on earth. How often does your inward focus influence the way you interact with others? In what ways does focusing inward impact your relationships with others?

3. Consider a situation in which you have felt awkward or out of place. How did the situation work out? Were you primarily focused on your insecurities, or were you watching for people to love? What is God showing you about his desire for you in similar situations?

4. Name one of your insecurities. In what ways would your life be different if this insecurity were no longer an influence on you?

5. What is God showing you about the power of looking outward as you aim to overcome your greatest insecurities? What step is he leading you to take as you follow him in this area?

Notes:

1. Freeman, E. P. (2019). *The next right thing : a simple, soulful practice for making life decisions*. Revell.

13

Grace for Weakness:

Creating Space for God to Move

Grace Takeaway: We lean into grace by letting God's power work through us in our weakest moments instead of building protective walls of human strength. From this posture, he will do a work of healing we could not do for ourselves, and he will draw others to Jesus in ways we could never draw them in our human strength.

I shared the story of my miscarriage in Chapter One, but I left out an important part of the story. I left out the part about sharing our hard, sad news with dozens of friends who knew we were expecting. Sharing the news was nothing short of gut-wrenching.

At the time, I was actively mentoring many younger women— women who are like younger sisters to me. I communicate with these women regularly, and we're honest about our lives. For this reason, many women knew that I was pregnant far before the "safe" sharing time at the end of the first trimester.

As the unfortunate events of the miscarriage unfolded, I realized I had the difficult job of sharing my painful update with every woman who knew that I was pregnant. With a broken heart, I sent texts, made phone calls, and told them what had happened.

Sharing the story while I was still living in the middle of it was tough. I admitted that I didn't have answers. I shared the truth while the grief was raw, and the edges of my heart were frayed.

About a week into the painful process of telling everyone, a close friend called me and said something that went like this: "Stacey, I think what you're doing is so brave. It's not easy to be vulnerable about the tough parts of your story when God's still in the middle of writing it. You're letting others see you in your weakness, and it is powerful."

To me, it just felt like I was doing what I had to do. I was telling people what was happening and showing up before I had neat and tidy answers about why it was happening. But I realized my friend was right. It takes courage to let others see our hearts in our vulnerable moments. Being honest about our weaknesses takes courage.

In his letter to the Corinthian church, the Apostle Paul wrote the following famous words: "And He has said to me, 'My grace is sufficient for you, for power is perfected in weakness.' Most gladly, therefore, I will rather boast about my weaknesses, so that the power of Christ may dwell in me" (2 Corinthians 12:9).

These familiar words remind us that our weakest moments create the perfect platforms for God to make his power known. I knew these words were true, but as my journey unfolded, I realized that it's far easier to memorize these words than to live them out when life falls apart.

As I mustered the courage to share the news of my miscarriage with one friend after another, part of me wanted to pretend I was strong and that I had all the answers about why we were facing our awful loss. I wanted to say that I was doing fine, summarize everything God was teaching me in three succinct sentences, and slap a red ribbon on top of the box containing my theology of suffering and death. However, I sensed God leading me down a different path. I sensed him leading me to be vulnerable with others instead of pretending to be fine or strong. I sensed him asking me to lean into his grace and let his power show up in my weakness.

Throughout the journey of grieving the miscarriage, God taught me several life-changing lessons about leaning into his grace in times of weakness. Let's begin by talking about the importance of finding our strength in Jesus' presence.

Find Your Strength in Jesus' Presence

Let's return to the sad moment I shared at the beginning of this book—the moment in our purple powder room when I realized I was losing our baby.

Do you remember the first step God led me to take on that cold winter morning? I sensed him inviting me to spend a few minutes pressing close to him before I turned to other people for help. Before calling my husband, mom, or closest friends, I went to the basement and shared my heart with Jesus first. During that time, I sorted through my emotions, let my mind settle, and created space for God's truth to wash over me.

In the days that followed, I continued to turn to Jesus for healing and strength. I often imagined him holding me in his arms as I rested in a quiet place or listened to worship music. I read Psalms, wrote in my journal, and prayed while taking long, slow walks outside.

The next time you feel weak or heartbroken, I encourage you to turn to Jesus for strength first. When we are weak and hurting, it's important to regularly set aside time and space to rest with him in silence and solitude. Imagine his arms around you, and let his love give you strength. It can also help to pour your heart out to the Lord by writing in your journal or praying out loud. If worshiping through music is healing for you, make time to soak in worship alone or with others. Meanwhile, spend time in God's Word daily and ask Jesus to strengthen you as his Word renews your mind. Also, spend time pursuing enjoyable activities with Jesus, as we discussed earlier in this book. All of these practices can help you find strength in Jesus.

It's also important to note that turning to Jesus first isn't an admonition to isolate ourselves. God designed us to live together in community and heal in community. As we turn to Jesus first, he will show us the select people he wants to use to help us grow stronger. We might refer to this group as an "inner circle" of trusted loved ones. Finding a trusted inner circle is an important part of the healing process, as well.

Find Your "Inner Circle"

My inner circle includes my husband, parents, sister, and a small group of close friends. These are the people with whom I know I'm safe to share the depths of my soul. They will speak words that build me up, point me to Christ, help me process my emotions, and honor my vulnerability by keeping my words in confidence. I can be transparent with them, and I trust that they know my heart and won't judge me.

We all need these trusted confidants in our lives. If you don't have one or two close friends or loved ones who can bear your greatest burdens with you, ask God to provide these people.

Jesus designed us to heal and find strength in community with others.

Including people with more life experience and wisdom in our inner circles is especially helpful. I'm thankful that God has provided my parents as well as several older women who can encourage me and offer strength and wisdom.

As you pray about finding these trusted mentors, consider looking for someone who makes you feel safe—someone with whom you can share your innermost desires, fears, and failures without feeling judged or ashamed. A good mentor will be a good listener. She will protect your confidence, and you won't feel worried that she might share your private thoughts with others. She will possess godly wisdom, and if it's a good fit, you will both enjoy spending time with one another. God designed us to live in intergenerational communities, and older, wiser women have much to offer.

The Lord has provided mentors in my life through colleagues at work, women's Bible studies, Christian writers' groups, and even within my own family. Sometimes, the support we need is closer than we realize. These women help us find strength in Christ and can be instrumental in our spiritual growth.

Now that we've explored what it might look like to find our inner circles, let's talk about sharing our weaknesses with people outside of these circles. For lack of a better phrase, we'll refer to these people as our "outer circles." Unlike sharing with our inner circles, when we share with our outer circles, we realize that these people aren't meant to become sources of strength; instead, God calls us to share our hearts so that his power can work through our weaknesses.

Offer Your "Outer Circle" the Gift of Vulnerability

As I worked through the emotions surrounding the miscarriage, I sensed that I was moving in the direction of strength and healing. I'd been grieving our loss in Jesus' presence, and I also knew it was time to tell the women who were not in my inner circle about our loss.

As I made phone calls, sent texts, and shared our difficult news, I was honest. I talked about grief and didn't gloss over my pain. I quickly noticed that sharing our sad news was opening the door to reveal my heart and to talk about the hope I have in Jesus—even in death.

Looking back, I see how God used my weakest moment to make his power known. By letting so many women see my broken heart, I offered them the gift of my vulnerable self—not the version of me that has all the pretty platitudes or the version that has rehearsed answers to the hard questions of life. Unlike showing up on a stranger's doorstep with a five-step plan for receiving Christ as Savior (not that there's anything wrong with door-to-door evangelism), I showed up in tears and weakness and talked about my Jesus, and this vulnerability built trust.

My vulnerability also created space for the light of Christ to shine through the cracks in my broken heart in a way that it does not shine from the mountaintops of strength and religious righteousness. Friends who were previously resistant to conversations about faith were suddenly open to talking about Jesus because my words came from a place of vulnerability and weakness. Some of the most powerful Jesus-centered conversations of my life took place in the weeks following the miscarriage because people are willing to listen when the platform is weakness instead of strength.

For years, I repeated the words, "His power is made perfect in my weakness," but I didn't know that weakness included emotional vulnerability. I thought this verse meant that God would give me supernatural energy when I felt tired, insight when I felt confused, direction when I was lost, and strength when I felt weak. All of these insights into his power are true, but God also wants to make his power known in our emotionally weak and vulnerable moments. These moments are often the perfect backdrop for his Spirit to move in power.

The voice of self-effort tells us to be strong and build walls to hide our brokenness from the world. Being vulnerable is scary.

Meanwhile, the voice of grace says, "Embrace these weaknesses. Weakness is the perfect platform for God to make his power known."

When we embrace our weaknesses as places where God wants to make his power known, we become vessels of his grace. Not only does God work within us, but he also works *through* us. His grace pours through us as his Spirit touches the hearts and minds of the people around us.

Telling so many people about the miscarriage wasn't a pleasant experience. It hurt. Sharing the story dozens of times was emotionally exhausting. However, in the years since it happened, several of the women who saw me in my pain have experienced miscarriages as well. Not surprisingly, I was the first person each of these women reached out to in their moments of loss. It broke my heart to know they were experiencing the same anguish I felt, but I also considered it a tremendous gift that they trusted me as a safe place to find hope.

Younger women don't come to my house with tears in their eyes and burdens on their hearts because they think I'm perfect. They come because they know I've walked through difficult times, too. They know I've wrestled with God and found him to be trustworthy, and they want me to help them discover the same truth. When this exchange takes place, God's grace flows through me to bring healing to these women. It's an act of grace

I could not perform on my own. And it's an act of grace that takes place only when I'm willing to let God's power move in my weakness.

In her book *You're Already Amazing*, Holley Gerth reminds us of God's perspective on our brokenness:

> You think you have to take what's broken and make it perfect in order to be used by me. But I think in a completely different way. I took what was perfect, my Son, and made him broken so that you could be whole. And because you belong to him, your brokenness can bring healing to others too.[1]

Handle Weakness with Patience and Grace

Before we conclude this chapter, I want to create space to talk about the importance of handling weaknesses with patience and grace. This is important because many people feel uncomfortable when others express weakness and vulnerability. With good intentions, they make unsympathetic remarks to relieve their discomfort.

Let's talk about what to do when we're on the receiving end of these remarks as well as how to avoid making hurtful and unsympathetic comments when others are weak and hurting.

When Others Lack Sympathy

Some people can't tolerate the discomfort of not being able to fix the pain others are experiencing. They show up at cemeteries and bedsides and offer unsympathetic cliches or monologues about all the reasons we should give thanks for our greatest losses. They have the best of intentions. They simply can't stand to sit with hurting friends and not be able to do a thing but cry together.

I experienced this scenario several times when I told others about our miscarriage. After I shared the sad news, a few friends immediately offered long discourses about how God would use my pain for good, reminded me that I now have a baby to meet in heaven, or elaborated on the ways I'll be able to minister to others from my pain. They were trying to be helpful and encouraging, but I wasn't ready for them to package my pain and put it neatly in a box.

As I faced these remarks, I reminded myself to extend grace to these friends. Many of them were younger women who simply hadn't learned to grieve alongside another person or express sympathy. They had sincere intentions and were trying to be supportive. I knew their hearts and reminded myself to receive their loving attempts to console me.

Meanwhile, these conversations reminded me that, often, the best gift we can offer grieving loved ones is the gift of sitting with them in their pain and not trying to fix the pain. In these moments, our loved ones don't need to hear three-point sermons or cliches. They need us to be present.

What does it look like to be present with someone who is hurting? Let's talk about how we can lovingly express sympathy and care when others are hurting.

How to be Sympathetic Toward Others

When our loved ones are hurting, we don't need to have all the right answers; we simply need to be available. For example, the week after the miscarriage, I called my mom at least once a day. I didn't always want to talk about my emotions. I called her because I longed for the comfort of her voice. Most of the time, we talked about the everyday moments of our lives. She always took a moment to ask how I was doing with our loss, but if I didn't feel like talking about it, we changed the topic and talked about the weather, the kids, or my dad's latest outdoor adventures. My mom was present, and her presence gave me strength and helped me heal.

In a similar sense, my husband often asked how my heart was doing. He created a safe space for me to cry, and he often sat with me on the couch and listened as I grieved our baby and mourned the loss of my many hopes and dreams for the years to come. In his wisdom, he didn't try to fix my pain or gloss over my grief. He was present.

The next time someone you love faces a loss or a season of weakness, remember that your presence is the greatest gift you can offer. Let me also gently offer a few phrases *not* to use in these situations:

"At least you still have . . ."

"Let me tell you how much worse this could be."

"Maybe God's trying to teach you . . ."

"It was just a game."

"It was just a dog."

"He was just a boyfriend."

"You'll feel better soon."

Instead of trying to come up with cheerful statements to alleviate the discomfort, the best gift is often the gift of crying with our hurting loved ones. It's the gift of staying close, even when our loved ones can't respond or thank us. Within the context of this closeness, God's love and power permeate life's weakest moments.

Questions for Reflection and Discussion:

1. Would you consider yourself a person who is comfortable opening up and sharing your weaknesses with others? Why or why not?

2. Do you feel comfortable when others open up to you in weak moments? Why or why not?

3. Has God ever asked you to be vulnerable with others when you were in the middle of your story—before you had answers or a grip on what was happening? How did you feel about sharing? How did it work out?

4. Why is it so important for us to find strength in Jesus instead of immediately running to other people in search of strength and hope?

5. Have you ever opened your heart to another person and received a trite cliché or uncompassionate rendition of a Bible verse? In what way does this kind of response push hurting people away from Jesus? How can you extend grace the next time someone responds to your vulnerability in this way?

Notes:

1. Gerth, H. (2012). *You're already amazing : embracing who you are, becoming all God created you to be*. Revell.

14

Grace for Life's Interruptions: Stewarding God's Assignments

Grace Takeaway: We lean into grace when we release the desire for control, give our best effort, and learn to trust God with the outcomes in our lives.

Every summer, I take our daughter Bekah on an overnight camping trip in Pennsylvania's forested hills. We shove our sleeping bags, tent, and provisions into my large, internal-frame backpack. We then strap the backpack to a double jogging stroller and fill the nooks and crannies of the stroller with everything from fishing poles to stuffed animals. I push our overloaded stroller miles into the wilderness, and we enjoy a night together in the woods. Wilderness camping with a little girl is nothing like the solo backpacking trips of my early twenties— it's about a thousand times better.

Recently, we returned home from our annual backpacking trip feeling tired and happy. We'd explored a new area, cooked s'mores over a smoky fire, and slept restlessly as we dreamed of black bears and raccoons. Little did we realize that our bodies were under attack as we slept beneath the hemlocks—just not by black bears.

The day after arriving home and unpacking our gear, I woke up feeling blessed to be in my bed and not lying on the hard ground. I felt rested, refreshed, and ready to tackle the new week. I had plans to take the kids to the library, visit the local bike path, finish editing a big writing project, and stock up on groceries.

I mentally planned the day as I stood at the kitchen sink to brew my morning pot of decaf. Distracted by an itchy abdomen, I scratched my waistline and assumed I must have fallen victim to a mosquito on our camping trip. As I pulled up my shirt to examine the bite, I could hardly believe my eyes. Five tiny ticks were embedded in my belly. I immediately thought of a friend who took her daughter camping at the same spot a year earlier. She texted me upon their return to report dozens of ticks all over their bodies.

"Oh no," I whispered as I used my fingernails to pry the tiny ticks from my flesh.

Pulling off my shirt and shorts in the middle of the kitchen, I began examining my body. Ticks were attached to my forearms, legs, feet, ankles, armpits, and places I dare not mention. Dozens of ticks.

Before finding the tweezers and getting to work on myself, I rushed to the living room to check on Bekah.

"Take your clothes off!" I urged her, panic welling inside me.

Looking at her partially clothed mama with a skeptical expression, my precious girl sighed, "Oh no. You found a tick, didn't you?"

"Not *a* tick," I muttered, "I found *many, many* ticks."

Sure enough, my sweet daughter was covered with ticks as well.

We spent the next hour sitting on the floor frantically picking ticks off of each other. By the time we'd removed every visible tick and scanned our bodies at least five times, I was in full-blown crisis mode.

I'd like to point out that I don't typically freak out over ticks. We spend a lot of time in the woods, and I find a tick embedded in one of the kids at least twice a month. I've learned to pull a tick out without leaving the head and legs in the skin. My research has also taught me that ticks don't typically transmit diseases if you pull them off within 48 hours. If you suspect a tick has been latched on for more than 48 hours, a quick trip to the doctor and a dose of antibiotics will prevent Lyme disease. We've never visited a doctor for a tick bite. We find them early, pull them off, and move on with our lives. No biggie.

The morning of the tick infestation was different. It *was* a big deal. We found at least 60 ticks attached to our bodies, and that's enough to make even the most rugged mountain woman come undone.

When Life Is Interrupted

We all face interruptions to our plans. In Chapter Four, we discussed adopting a "Now What?" mentality when our daily plans take a detour. Today, we'll talk about bigger interruptions—those interruptions that threaten to derail our lives for weeks, months, or even years.

I understand that our tick infestation was not as big of an interruption as a chronic diagnosis, shattered marriage, lost job, or the death of a loved one. However, I share this story because God used it to show me how to lean into his grace when an interruption to my plans feels out of control.

Return with me to the morning of the tick infestation, and we'll explore a mindset that can help us cope with life's interruptions.

After Bekah and I removed the ticks from our bodies, I attempted to resume my quiet devotional time with the Lord. I sat down, placed my Bible on my lap, and took a few minutes to calm my nervous system by breathing slowly.

After a few minutes of deep breathing, I felt more rational and decided to calculate exactly how many hours had passed since we arrived at our camping spot. I counted 40 hours since setting up camp. If the ticks started latching on when we first got there, we were cutting it close to the 48-hour safety window. We were at risk for Lyme disease, and I needed to call the doctor.

As is often the case when I consider visiting the doctor, I began assessing our options. Should we go to Urgent Care or visit our primary care physician? Which would cost less? Maybe I could just make a phone call and get a script for a prescription without visiting the office. I might need to call my mom to watch the boys. An ongoing stream of questions scrolled through my spinning head.

Feeling overwhelmed, I searched my Bible for a verse about surrendering to God's plans. My search led me to 1 Peter 4:10, which reads, "As each one has received a special gift, employ it in serving one another as stewards of the multifaceted grace of God."

Immediately, one phrase from the verse seemed to leap off the page: "serving one another as stewards."

"God, what would it look like to be a good steward of your grace in this situation?" I prayed.

As I reflected on the idea of stewardship, I recognized that being a good steward in our situation meant calling the doctor, making appointments, scrapping my schedule, and caring for our bodies.

Within a few hours, Bekah and I were both under our doctor's care with instructions to watch our tick bites and monitor our symptoms. With preventative antibiotics in our bodies, we seemed to have averted immediate disaster.

Give Your Best and Trust God with the Outcome

The following morning, I sat by the window and reflected on the events of the previous day. Knowing I had been a good steward by taking steps to care for our bodies brought a sense of peace, but I was still concerned that we might have already contracted Lyme disease as the result of so many tick bites. I worried we might get sick or suffer long-term effects from the disease.

"Lord, I feel fearful and shaken," I prayed. "Please lead me to truth to stand on today."

I then opened my journal and wrote the following words:

Stacey, your role is to give your best in every situation God places in front of you, but remember that the outcomes of these situations are not yours to control. God calls you to be a faithful steward of his work, and he wants you to trust him with the results.

Peace settled over me as I reminded myself that I had been a faithful steward of our bodies. The outcome was in God's hands.

In John 15, Jesus offers a metaphor and describes God as a vine. We are branches on this vine, and when we remain close to the vine, our lives will bear fruit. When we stay close to God, doing our best with the daily work he sets before us, we can trust God with the results (the fruit). These results include the physical outcomes in our situations, but they also include the fruit that springs up in our souls—fruits such as joy and peace.

I invite you to consider the areas of your life in which joy and peace are lacking. Do you notice a correlation between trying to hold onto control and experiencing a lack of joy and peace? Conversely, do you notice any correlation between surrendering to God in trust and experiencing the peace that surpasses understanding?

As we contemplate these realms of our lives, I'd like to take a moment to examine the difference between stewardship and control.

The Difference Between Stewardship and Control

Most of us think about finances and material possessions when we hear the word "stewardship." However, biblical stewardship extends far beyond finances. Biblical stewardship is managing *all* of God's resources for his glory, which ultimately results in our well-being.[1]

God's resources include our finances and material possessions; however, God is also calling us to be good stewards of the everyday tasks he places in front of us.

This daily work includes caring for loved ones, maintaining our homes, tending to our pets, calling our friends, serving in our churches, and undertaking the thousands of large and small responsibilities that fill our days.

This work also includes dealing with life's unpleasant interruptions: listening to disgruntled coworkers, serving grouchy clients, attending to our bodies in times of illness and physical distress, and navigating crises of every form.

When God permits unpleasant interruptions, most of us respond by trying to gain a sense of control. Instead of remembering that God is sovereign over the challenging situations we face, we stress ourselves out in our attempts to orchestrate our desired results.

I know about this desire for control because I've spent most of my life trying to control the circumstances God places in front of me. I have the best of intentions. Self-effort tells me to make sure no one in my life has to face pain or discomfort. This desire manifests itself in a variety of ways: I always overpack when our family embarks on weekend adventures; I'm obsessed with hand sanitizer; by Sunday evenings, I generally have a loose plan for our weekly dinner menu; and I stay organized with lists.

At first glance, these behaviors seem wise. There's nothing wrong with being prepared or having clean hands! However, I have been known to be so stressed out about packing for a weekend adventure that the stress overshadows the joy of the journey. I've also been known to turn to my lists for peace instead of turning to Christ as my source of peace.

Perhaps you have a strong urge to control certain areas of your life, too. You might try to control what people think about you by being funny, sarcastic, or intellectual. Maybe you're careful to never leave the house without makeup, and you wouldn't dare go to the store in your sweats. Your control issues might center on your career, your kids, your marriage, your friendships, or your use of time.

Much to our dismay, we all face times when life feels out of control. We realize we're infested with ticks, lice, mice, or termites. We realize we don't have the money to pay the bills.

We reach the end of our ropes and feel like we're losing the strength to hold on. In these moments, we lean into God's grace by opening our clenched fists, doing the best we can, and leaving the outcomes in God's hands. We remember that when we stay close to the vine, we can trust that our lives will bear good fruit (John 15).

There is freedom in reaching the end of a stressful day, sinking into your bed, and wholeheartedly saying, "I did my best, and the outcome is up to you, Lord."

Being a good steward of today's God-given task might look like setting aside your goals at work and staying home with your sick child. God might call you to spend the time, money, and energy to take yourself to the doctor and care for your body. Perhaps God is encouraging you to do the best you can to care for the precious loved one who is fighting a battle between life and death—all while remembering that the outcome is not in your hands.

No matter what we are facing, stewardship involves doing our best and trusting God with the results.

When I think about trusting God with parts of my life that are important to me, I vividly remember a season that challenged us all. The year was 2020, and the whole world was trying to figure out how to navigate a "new normal" as we faced a global pandemic. I invite you to join our family as we endured the lockdown and reflect on the ways the pandemic challenged you to release control and trust God, too.

Trusting God with the Results

In the fall of 2020, our region's local public schools closed their doors to protect our children and our community from illness. I was suddenly responsible for overseeing Bekah's fourth-grade studies, teaching Caleb everything that kindergarteners are expected to master by the end of the year (including learning to read), and caring for one-year-old Aiden. Like so many parents, the responsibility of teaching my kids was added to an already full life of writing, caring for our home, and keeping tabs on other loved ones.

Because I have a teaching degree and spent close to a decade as a high school special education teacher, when the school shut down, many well-meaning friends and family members remarked, "This should be a breeze for you! You've spent enough years in the classroom that teaching your own kids should be easy for you!"

Sadly, these friends were very wrong.

When I was a high school teacher, teaching students who did *not* live in my home was enjoyable and fulfilling. My students generally respected me and listened to me.

Teaching my own children was different.

Day after day, Caleb and I worked on learning to read. Most days, we were interrupted by Aiden as he climbed onto the kitchen table in the middle of our lessons, attempted to eat crayons, wailed from the living room, or banged on pots and pans.

Meanwhile, Bekah was mostly left to fend for herself while completing her assignments upstairs on her laptop. I tried to check in on her work, but I was so overwhelmed that many days, I didn't have the time to invest much energy reviewing her daily lessons.

On many days, we all shed tears.

I cried because I was frustrated and overwhelmed, but I also cried because I felt like I was failing my kids. I feared that Bekah and Caleb would fall behind in school, and their lives would be forever marred by their tired mother's ineptitude.

I felt like I was failing little Aiden because I wasn't giving him the attention he deserved. We were supposed to be reading storybooks and embarking on adventures together while his older siblings were in school. Instead, we were all just trying to survive.

In addition, my husband continued to work long hours throughout the entire pandemic. By the time he arrived home each evening, we were all exhausted, which meant that saving schoolwork for evenings wasn't practical for our family.

Somewhere in the middle of the school year, I found a quiet moment to talk to God and share my fears with him. After telling him everything I was feeling, I sat in silence and asked him to show me what I needed to know about the calling he had set before me.

In response, a quiet impression settled upon my heart: I recognized that I was doing my best; the outcome was not mine to control.

Immediately, I recognized the significance of this truth. As every wise parent knows, we are called to do our best to raise our children, but their lives are not ours to control. Their failures are not ours to claim, and neither are their successes.

In the weeks following that difficult moment, I recognized that God was calling me to new levels of trust. My role was to do my best to navigate the pandemic and teach our kids, but God never asked me to take control of the outcomes in my children's lives.

In the same way, God wants us to learn to trust him with our dreams, our careers, our futures, and the people we cherish. Meanwhile, here's the tricky part of the process when it comes to learning to trust God: Just as we learn to be patient in patience-testing situations, God teaches us to trust him by putting us in situations that challenge our trust in him.

I wish I could snap my fingers and miraculously develop a heart that completely trusts God all the time. However, that's not how trust works. We build trust through experience. In the same way that we don't learn to trust new friends overnight, our trust in God grows with time and experience.

God places us in circumstances that feel out of control, and these circumstances are his classrooms for developing deeper trust. These situations rarely feel pleasant when we're in the middle of them. God turns our five-year plans upside down and shuts down our great dreams. He often allows uncertainty to lead us into his arms, and he offers his presence without offering clarity.

These situations offer an invitation: We can choose to fight for a sense of control and security, or we can be faithful stewards of whatever God sets in front of us. We can trust that when we do our part to wholeheartedly undertake for the work set before us, God will bring *his* purposes to pass (Psalm 37:5).

Nevertheless, at times we will undertake our God-given assignments to the best of our abilities and face disappointing results. Here are a few examples: You might put forth excellent effort at your job, and you might still get fired; you might be a loving and godly wife, but you might still end up divorced; you might pour your heart into teaching your kids to make good decisions, but they will still make painful mistakes.

It's important to remember that we can do our best—and even work with excellence—and be met with devastating results. This realization is tough to swallow, but it also frees us from the stress of trying to manage what was never ours to control.

I close this chapter with a question: In which area of your life is God inviting you to stop trying to take control and, instead, trust that your best effort is enough?

Your heavenly Father wants to help you grow in trust. Ask him to deepen your trust in him, and he will answer your prayer. His answer will most likely come in the form of situations in which trusting him feels difficult, but you can walk forward in peace when you know that you've given your best effort. The results are in his trustworthy hands.

Questions for Reflection and Discussion:

1. Do any areas of your life feel out of control? In what ways have you been responding to these situations? In what ways have you been trying to gain control and orchestrate positive outcomes?

2. What concrete steps can you take to be a good steward of the most challenging assignment in your life? List these steps below or in a journal and be as specific as possible. What is God asking from you when it comes to giving your best effort and trusting him with the outcome in this situation?

3. Describe a time in the past when God was trustworthy in a difficult situation. In what way does this memory of God's faithfulness strengthen you as you consider your current trials?

4. In what ways does a stewardship mentality shift the focus from our human abilities to God's divine plan? How does this mentality make you feel?

Notes:

1. *Stewardship in the Bible - Definition and Examples*. (n.d.). Christianity.com. https://www.christianity.com/wiki/christian-terms/stewards-in-the-bible-meaning-of-stewardship.html#google_vignette

15

Grace for Relationships:

Extending Grace to the People We Love

Grace Takeaway: We lean into grace when we create space for God to work in our relationships by holding our loved ones with care and gentleness.

My husband often tells our son Caleb to "treat Mom like a baby peep." The first time he spoke these words, I didn't understand their significance. At the time, Caleb was a toddler. He was energetic and playful; he was also too small to hurt me by climbing on me or crashing into me.

Several years have passed, and now I understand the value of my husband's admonition. Caleb has doubled in size and likes to stampede through the house roaring like a lion. He's getting bigger and stronger, and he could easily hurt me by diving onto me or attempting to wrestle with me. He means no harm and loves me dearly; he simply needs the reminder to treat me like a baby peep—softly and gently—on a regular basis.

I don't know if you've held a fluffy yellow chick recently (if you haven't, you should), but consider the way you need to hold a chick. The chick needs enough space to wiggle in your hand and breathe. It needs to be held in a way that offers gentle care while also allowing room for it to move.

We've spent the past 14 chapters learning how to lean into God's grace, allowing him to work in our lives to accomplish what we cannot accomplish through self-effort. Today, we'll explore a principle to help us carry God's grace into our relationships: learning to hold our relationships gently—in the same way we would hold baby peeps.

The work God does in our lives is not meant to be an end in itself. Just as God fills us with love so that we can go into the world and love others, he offers his grace so that we might become people who offer grace to others. When we learn to hold our relationships gently, we leave room for God to work and move—in our lives and in the lives of our loved ones.

There are two sides to holding our relationships gently. On one side, if we squeeze too tightly—forcing our loved ones to conform to our expectations—we will smother our relationships. No relationship can thrive when the life is squeezed out of it.

On the other side, if we hold our relationships too loosely and fail to provide the necessary care, our lack of attention will hurt our loved ones, and our relationships will fail to flourish.

Some of us tend to hold our relationships too tightly by expecting more than our loved ones are able to give and wasting valuable energy feeling hurt and offended. We also hold our relationships too tightly when try to act as the Holy Spirit in the lives of our friends and spouses, hoping to help them change instead of leaving their transformation in God's hands.

I tend to fall into the category of those who hold relationships too loosely. I am an introvert, and too much pressure in relationships overwhelms me and pushes me away. At times, I forget that some of my friends need more care and attention than I am naturally inclined to offer. I might feel like a friendship is thriving when we text each other weekly and get together once a month. However, some of my friends need more than this to feel cared for and lovingly tell me when my distance is hurtful. In these friendships, it's important for me to make sure I'm not holding the relationship *too* loosely.

Today, we'll explore how to let God's grace transform our relationships. We'll talk about how to extend grace in our friendships, and then I'll share my testimony about extending grace to my husband.

I now invite you to join me at my kitchen table as I share the story of a recent conflict with a friend.

Extending Grace in Our Friendships

It's a sunny spring afternoon, and I sit at the kitchen table with my phone in hand. I'm praying about how to respond to a text I received from a friend.

Hold this gently—like a baby peep, my husband's voice echoes in my mind.

A few hours ago, a friend who lives a few hours away sent me a message telling me that she will be coming to town and wants to see me. She suggested Friday afternoon between 2:00 and 4:00 and told me that she hoped to stop by my house to catch up.

Unfortunately, I have a big writing deadline on Saturday. I've been going back and forth with my editor all week, and our family's afternoon quiet time is the time of day when I write. It's the only time of day when our house is quiet enough for me to write coherently. This is the precise time of the day when my friend wants to visit. I know that I'll need to be writing at that time to meet my deadline.

Prayerfully, I send my friend a message explaining the situation and asking if she can meet me at a different time.

Within seconds the phone vibrates. She responds with the following words: "Why do you have to use 2:00 to 4:00 as your writing time every day? Maybe you could shift things around for just one day."

Oh, dear. I've hurt her feelings, I think. Picking up the phone, I send another message explaining why I have to write during our daily quiet time and explain the importance of quiet children in order to focus on writing.

"I see. Maybe another time then," she responds.

My heart sinks as I read her curt response. I immediately realize that this difficult conversation is more than an issue of scheduling. It's an issue of desire. My friend would rearrange her schedule to make a visit work if I were visiting her town. The fact that I'm not willing to make the same adjustment has hurt her feelings. Perhaps she feels like I don't value the relationship as much as she does.

Recognizing all of this, I call her so that we can talk in person. I tell her how much I love, appreciate, and value her. I ask her to give me a little more warning—if possible—before her next visit and assure her that I will do my best to make her a priority.

We both share our hearts; the conversation isn't easy. Being honest about our feelings and expectations makes us both feel vulnerable. However, we create space for understanding and grace, and our friendship has been stronger since that day.

My friend has given me permission to share this story about our misunderstanding, and we pray it helps you grasp the importance of holding your friendships with care and gentleness.

I didn't feel gently held by my friend. Instead, I felt like her expectations had me pressed into a tight spot, and there wasn't much room for grace. My friend didn't understand that my writing work includes deadlines and that I need to sit down to focus on writing work every single day.

In the same way that a teacher, nurse, or lawyer can't just leave her workplace for an impromptu afternoon visit, I can't ignore my work every time a friend comes to town. My friend didn't understand my reality (or maybe she thinks we're close enough that she should be an exception to my boundaries), and as a result, her feelings were hurt.

I share this example because it recently took place in my life. This time, I was the friend who felt too tightly squeezed by my friend's expectations; however, at other times, I have been the friend with high expectations and hurt feelings.

How can we hold our friendships gently and leave room for God's grace to move within these relationships? Let's talk about how to respond when our friends fail to meet our expectations, and then we'll explore positive responses for times when we feel like our friends are holding us too tightly.

How to Respond When Your Expectations Aren't Met

One lesson I have learned over time is that repeatedly pointing out where my friends are failing to meet my expectations does not produce healthy relationships. Some people are simply unable to live up to our expectations.

When I realize that I'm consistently disappointed by a friend who doesn't have time for me or doesn't respond to my messages, I ask myself a few questions.

First, I consider whether my expectations are realistic. Maybe this friend just started a new job, had a baby, or is dealing with a crisis. Perhaps she has a full schedule without much margin. I'm careful to listen closely when she shares the details of her life, and I often realize that she is not able to meet my expectations. If this is the case, I extend grace and try to focus on how I can support her instead of focusing on what she can offer to me.

Second, I consider whether my friend's actions are simply a part of her unique personality or might be an area where she has room for growth. For example, I have a few friends who aren't good at responding to text messages. I used to feel hurt by these friends, but I've learned not to take offense. They aren't good at keeping up with their phones, and this has nothing to do with me. Analyzing their behavior or stressing out over how I might have offended them is never helpful. Instead of overthinking their delayed responses, I let it go and have even learned to laugh about it. If I want to talk to them, I call them.

I could choose to pull away from these friends, and there is a time for that. If you feel like you're the only one reaching out in a friendship, God might be telling you to invest your energy elsewhere. However, he might also be telling you that your friend's poor communication isn't really about you at all. In these situations, ask God to direct you. He might reveal the reason for your friend's behavior or show you a creative way to stay connected.

Third, when a friend fails to meet my expectations, I ask myself if I'm turning to my friend to meet my emotional needs at a time when God wants me to turn to him. In certain seasons, I was consistently hurt by unmet expectations within relationships because I expected other people to fill emotional and spiritual needs that only God can fill.

We all face the temptation to turn to other people instead of turning to God to meet our needs. A phone call to a friend often *feels like* it is producing more immediate and measurable results than talking to God. God wants us to live in relationships with others and bear one another's burdens, but he also wants us to learn to turn to *him* to fulfill our relational needs and desires.

231

Often, when I feel disappointed in human relationships, my disappointment stems from the fact that I expected another person to meet a need that only God could meet.

Lastly, I've learned that friendships go through seasons. There's an ebb and flow to most friendships. For example, maybe your best friend is facing a major transition in her life. You feel hurt that she doesn't have much time for you now. You're considering writing her off.

Please, don't write her off.

I've been the friend in transition, and most likely, your friend still loves and values you. Her season has changed, and yours hasn't.

Hold her gently.

Extend grace, even when you don't understand what's happening in your friendship. Remind yourself that in five years, the flow of your friendship might lead you back together, closer than ever.

As friends move in and out of your life—and then in and out again—you can trust God with his timing. Love them when they come and love them when they go. You will find joy within these friendships, and this will help them flourish.

My deepest, healthiest friendships are with women who are good at holding our friendships gently. We've learned to ride the tide of dozens of seasons in life, and at the end of the day, I know these women are there for me. The friendships that last are the ones that have learned the secret of leaving room for grace.

How to Respond When Others Hold You Too Tightly

Now, let's consider the times when the shoe is on the other foot. How should we respond when we're not able to meet our friends' expectations, and we feel like we're being held too tightly?

First, turning to God in prayer can help us respond with grace. God knows what's going on in the lives of our loved ones, and he wants to give us wisdom. Instead of talking to other people about the friend who is squeezing you too tightly, talk to God. Create space to listen for anything he might want to reveal to you. He wants to show you how to respond to your friend.

After praying about the issue, God might lead you to reach out and ask for insight from a wise person in your life. Explaining the situation to a mature believer and asking for advice can give you insight into how to move forward. It's important to note that seeking wise counsel is not the same as venting to your husband or your other friends. This kind of venting often leads to gossiping and doesn't promote a soft and grace-filled response.

Second, consider alternate ways to reach out to your friend while still respecting your boundaries. Is there a different time or place where you could meet? Would a phone call work instead of meeting face-to-face?

Additionally, consider whether there is a pattern within this friendship. Is this the only time your friend has ever asked for more than you feel capable of giving, or is this a conversation you've had a dozen times? If there isn't a pattern of feeling too tightly held by this friend, then perhaps God is asking you to reach out to meet her need and break a boundary for this specific situation. However, if you frequently have this conversation with your friend, then it might be time to be very honest with her about your limits and your availability.

Lastly, after talking to God and considering different ways of meeting your friend's needs, go directly to her and talk it out. My dad has given me many wise pieces of advice throughout my life. One of the best pieces of advice he has offered is that when relational conflicts arise, we should always, "Go to the source."

Share your heart with your friend. Tell her how much you value her friendship, and then explain the constraints of your current season in life. Perhaps she doesn't realize that you're emotionally and physically exhausted and have been working long hours. Maybe she hasn't considered how demanding the summer months are with all of your children or grandchildren home on summer break. Offer suggestions for ways to make your friendship work, even if you have to resort to phone calls or late-evening coffee shop dates for a season.

Sadly, some friends want more than we are able to offer them. If this is the case with your friend, she might gradually distance herself from you, or she might get angry and break off your friendship. These situations are heart-wrenching. God uses relational conflicts to help us grow, and there aren't formulas or clear-cut answers for navigating complex relationships. However, I have learned that I can walk in peace when I apply the truth we learned earlier in this book to my friendships: I do my best to be a good friend and trust God with the results.

I pray these insights will help you learn to hold your friends with gentle hands. Let's now shift gears and talk about leaving room for God's grace to work in our romantic relationships.

Extending Grace in Romantic Relationships

Just as important as holding our friendships gently, our romantic relationships thrive when we learn to leave room for God's grace. Early in our marriage, before my husband and I had learned effective ways to express our frustrations, desires, and unmet expectations, we sometimes had conversations about what the other person could do better as a spouse. This kind of open communication can benefit a marriage, but it can also be destructive, especially if the communication feels condemning.

Unfortunately, our conversations usually carried a tone of frustration and negativity instead of love and grace. Every time we had one of these conversations, I felt a paralyzing sense of condemnation and felt like a failure as a wife.

When we were first married, one of our biggest issues was the difference between our expressions of affection. I came from a home in which acts of service were the most frequent ways of expressing love and care. My husband was raised in an affectionate home where hugs and close physical contact were the most common expressions of love.

As a result of our very different upbringings, I often felt unloved when my husband overlooked household tasks that were important to me. If he left a messy kitchen for me to clean, didn't mow the lawn, or forgot to take out the garbage, I felt uncared for. Meanwhile, when I failed to hug, cuddle, and reach out to him with affection, he felt unloved.

We both failed to hold our relationship gently every time we initiated critical conversations about these differences.

Over time, the Lord began to show us both that the negative conversations weren't helping our marriage. Instead, the hard conversations were suffocating our marriage because we were trying to force one another into molds that didn't fit.

By constantly harping on the areas where the other person was failing, we both felt discouraged and immobilized. The conversations were paralyzing because any small growth was overshadowed by looming inner voices that mocked, *You're still not doing enough! You'll never be good enough in this area!* Instead of continuing to move in the direction of meeting one another's needs, we felt defeated and incapable of changing.

With time, maturity, and receptivity to God's work in our lives, God began working in our hearts and shifting our focus. Instead of focusing on what the other person lacked, we started to appreciate what we each brought into our marriage. We learned that our differences created balance and saw this balance as a gift from God.

I'm grateful that my loving husband has learned to hold me gently, and I aim to follow his Christlike example and hold him gently as well. For example, he encourages me when I succeed at showing affection, and he doesn't lecture me or make me feel like I'm failing him when I'm not as cuddly as he'd prefer. He winks at me when I reach out to hold his hand and thanks me when I express my love through physical expressions.

We've learned to laugh about our differences instead of being critical. I've learned that when he leaves muddy boot prints on the floor or doesn't take the garbage out, he's not intentionally trying to create more work for me. I've learned to extend grace and realize that he either forgot, was in a hurry, or was exhausted.

We're growing.

Do you want more joy in your marriage or your romantic relationship? Hold your loved one gently. Don't make him feel like a failure when he doesn't live up to your expectations. Learn to laugh about the idiosyncrasies that get under your skin. Flavor your conversations with humor and lightheartedness instead of pride and seriousness. Any time you catch yourself lecturing him, stop. Your lectures won't have the desired result.

Also, don't assume that your expectations for your relationship are right and that his ideas are wrong. God created us uniquely, and differences bring balance into our marriages. Learning to appreciate these differences strengthens our marriages.

Lastly, God calls us to build up our spouses, but he does not ask us to step into the role of the Holy Spirit in their lives. We can trust God to work in the lives of our loved ones in his timing. He is fully capable of speaking to their hearts, and he shapes their hearts in his timing—not ours.

My husband and I are both very different people from the 20-somethings we were when we said our marriage vows. God's grace has softened us, shaped us, and filled our marriage with greater joy and love than we ever imagined. Leave room for God's grace to work in your marriage, and he can transform this relationship beyond your greatest expectations.

Questions for Reflection and Discussion:

1. Ask God to remind you of a time when someone extended grace to you in a challenging situation. What did this situation teach you about extending grace to others?

2. We all feel tempted to turn to other people instead of turning to God to meet our emotional needs at times. When do you feel most tempted to turn to other people instead of turning to God to meet your needs? What is God showing you about his desire to meet these needs?

3. Ask God to show you if you have taken offense because you feel too tightly held by someone in your life. Return to the steps I suggested for navigating this situation and ask God to show you how to respond to this situation. What is God showing you? In what way is he calling you to respond in this situation?

4. In what ways is the Lord inviting you to extend grace to your spouse or significant other in response to this chapter's insights? Have you ever tried to play the role of the Holy Spirit in this person's life? How did that turn out for you? What is God showing you about loving your significant other and letting him work in your loved one's life in his perfect timing?

16

Grace for the Sting of Rejection:
Taking a Stand Against Shame

Grace Takeaway: We lean into grace when rejection leads us to the freedom of growth instead of leading us to the condemnation of shame.

As I sit to write this last chapter, my heart overflows with gratitude for you, dear friend. Together, we've traveled over the mountaintops and through the valleys of our lives. We've learned how to bring our fears, insecurities, and broken hearts to the Lord so that his grace can heal us.

As we draw near to the end of our time together, we'll explore one final way to experience God's grace: walking with God when we've been rejected in areas of our lives that are deeply important to us.

Today, I invite you to join me as I share the story of a heartbreaking rejection, and we'll talk about how to grow through rejection instead of being controlled by the shame that may arise in these challenging situations.

The Death of My Dream

Before I share this story with you, I must admit that it's a difficult story for me to retell. Nevertheless, there is redemption in this story. When I reflect on the way God has used this painful rejection for my good and his glory, I am inspired and filled with gratitude.

My story began on a warm spring afternoon when a world-renowned company hired me to work for them as a writer. I had been dreaming of turning writing into a career, and my dream had finally come to fruition.

I was immediately assigned an enormous project, and I spent six months pouring my whole heart into the project. The work was satisfying and purposeful, and I loved it. At times it was demanding, but most of the time, I felt fulfilled—like I was doing what God had created me to do.

As I pursued my new career, our family made the necessary adjustments. We rearranged our lives so that I could meet deadlines; we even planned vacations around my schedule. The sacrifices were difficult at times, but we were determined to make it work.

Shortly before the culmination of the large project, everything seemed to be going well. My coworkers commended me for my work, and my future with the company seemed bright. Then, on a sunny autumn afternoon, a phone call turned my world upside down.

The woman on the other end of the phone began by thanking me for my excellent work ethic and for being a team player. She then dropped a bomb. The company had decided to terminate me, and they would be discarding the project I had worked on for the past six months.

I'll spare you the details, but the short version of the story is that the company recognized a disparity between my biblical core beliefs and their core beliefs. They didn't want me to be a part of their organization, and they had decided to let me go.

I was crushed. The many months of work, the sleepless nights, the family sacrifices, the emotional energy—it suddenly felt like it was all for nothing. To say I was disappointed would be a drastic understatement. I was devastated.

I had been rejected in a place that mattered deeply to me. I felt like I had failed. On one level, I knew that standing for my biblical core beliefs is never a failure, but on a different level, the voice of shame told me that I lost the job because I was not good enough. This voice said, *You were never a good enough writer to work for them. Why did you even try? You should be so embarrassed about this. You have failed. How foolish of you to chase this writing dream!*

I wanted to crawl into a corner and hide from the world, and the thought of telling my friends and family that I'd lost the job made me feel sick inside. I knew that pride was feeding the shame I felt; nevertheless, the shame was paralyzing.

Most of us will face rejection. Sometimes, rejection looks like a shattered dream or the loss of a job. At other times, it comes from people we care about. Friends betray us or decide they don't want to remain friends. Marriages fall apart. Close family members—including parents, siblings, and children—push us away.

These rejections hurt.

When we're rejected, we face a choice: We can learn and grow as a result of the rejection, or we can let shame paralyze and control us.

It's tempting to give in to the voice of shame. This voice tells us there's something wrong with us, we're lacking, or we don't measure up. Shame tells us to take necessary measures to ensure that the word doesn't see us for the failures we truly are. We might feel paralyzed, which leads us to withdraw, numb ourselves, or give up. At other times, shame leads us to overcompensate by finding ways to prove—to ourselves and others—that we're not failures. This might look like jumping into a new relationship before taking the time to heal from a divorce or setting out on search for a "new best friend" after a friendship falls apart. It might look like trying to redeem a shattered dream in our own strength instead of grieving the loss and waiting for God to open the next door.

Meanwhile, Jesus offers a different, more life-giving invitation. Instead of listening to the voice of shame, he invites us to draw near to him, share our emotions with him, and let him help us grow through life's most painful rejections. Rejection is one of the most painful human experiences; however, it can also be one of the greatest springboards for emotional and spiritual growth.

We're going to spend the remainder of this chapter learning how to respond to rejection in such a way that it becomes a life-changing tool that God can use to help us grow in grace, love, and community. We'll talk about drawing near to God when we've been rejected, resisting the inclination to hold onto offense, bringing shame into the light with others, and watching for God's better plan.

Let's revisit the afternoon when I lost my writing job, and we'll talk about drawing near to God when we've been rejected.

Drawing Near to God Amid Rejection

After losing my writing job, I went for a long walk and attempted to talk through my emotions with Jesus. Dozens of thoughts and feelings raced through my heart and mind.

I lacked direction about where to go next with my writing career, and most of me wanted to quit writing altogether. I was angry and hurt. I felt rejected and confused.

As I wrestled with my mixed emotions, I prayed a simple prayer. "Lord, show me what you want me to know about all of this," I whispered.

I've discovered that this prayer, "Show me what you want me to know," is among the most powerful prayers I can pray. God knows things we don't know, and he wants to reveal the truth to us.

In response to my prayer, God didn't impress a clear thought upon my mind or remind me of a verse to encourage me. Instead, I imagined Jesus holding me, his tenderness engulfing me. I felt loved, seen, and above all else, known.

As painful as it was, I sensed that losing the job was Jesus' form of protection. I didn't understand what he was doing at first, but I knew he was offering me an invitation to trust him.

As I considered what it might look like to trust Jesus, I thought of Proverbs 3:5-6, which reads, "Trust in the Lord with all your heart and do not lean on your own understanding. In all your ways acknowledge Him, and He will make your paths straight."

God's Word washed over me, and I spontaneously whispered, "I trust you, Jesus—even when I don't understand."

As I soaked in the words of truth, an outpouring of joy swept over me. Flooded with the sense of Jesus' pleasure, I leaned into his presence and let his joy strengthen my heart.

At that moment, my encounter with Jesus began to dispel my shame. I recognized that what felt like a failure was actually the Lord's way of protecting me from walking down a path that wasn't best for my life. Less than a year later, his better plan would manifest itself in brilliant glory.

I'll share the details of God's better plan for my writing career at the end of the chapter. First, let's take a moment to talk about the times when rejection sends us reeling in pain, and we have no sense of Jesus' presence with us.

I want to encourage you not to be discouraged if you draw near to Jesus and don't sense his presence. We all experience Jesus differently, and when we have no sense of his presence with us, his Word is the anchor for our souls.

When I don't sense anything from the Lord, I remind myself that feelings are meant to be felt, but they're not strong enough to stand on. Instead of letting myself get caught up in my feelings, I turn to God's Word and find a promise to stand on.

It helps to specifically name the emotion I'm feeling so that I can find a biblical promise that will directly speak truth to the lie I am believing. For example, if a friend doesn't seem to have time for me, I might realize that I'm feeling unlovable or unworthy. I then search the Bible to find truth that affirms my true identity as God's child. I might stand on the promise of Romans 8:39, which reminds me that nothing in all creation can separate me from the love of my heavenly Father. I then speak these words every time I feel unlovable. Over time, God uses this discipline to renew my mind.

Appendix A in the back of this book contains 99 promises about our identities as God's children. I encourage you to turn to this resource often, meditate on these truths, and practice standing on God's promises instead of standing on your emotions.

In addition to drawing near to God, we can grow through rejection by resisting the urge to take offense or blame God for our disappointing circumstances. According to Jesus' words, when we choose not to take offense during times of hardship, we are blessed.

The Blessing of Remaining Unoffended

Several years ago, I made a radical commitment to God. I told him that I would never again take offense, blame him, or hold it against him when trouble came into my life.

I made the commitment at the end of a long season in which everything seemed to be going wrong. Within the span of three months, both of our young pet beagles died suddenly; our financial situation suddenly became unstable; my husband was diagnosed with a life-long medical condition; and I faced a serious health scare.

After months of stress and worry—when I felt like I couldn't take one more crisis—I went to the woods and told God how I felt. I complained. I told him it was all unfair and held nothing back.

I also asked God what he wanted me to know about our troubling series of events. Much to my disappointment, God seemed silent, and I had no sense of his presence with me. I knew he hadn't abandoned me, but it sure felt like it. When I needed him most, there was no sign that he even heard my prayers.

Several days later, I opened my Bible for my daily morning reading, and the bookmarked page led me to Matthew 11. After reading the passage about John the Baptist being sent to prison and questioning whether Jesus was the Messiah, the following words seemed to leap off the page: "And blessed is the one who is not offended by me" (Matthew 11:6, ESV).

Immediately, I knew that God was offering me a choice. I could hold a grudge while blaming him for the trials he'd permitted in my life, or I could choose to trust him, soften my heart, and resist offense.

It didn't happen immediately, but I spent the following weeks asking God to help me trust him with our challenging circumstances. Every day, when worried thoughts came into my mind, I repeated the words of Isaiah 26:3, which reads, "You will keep in perfect peace those whose minds are steadfast, because they trust in you" (NIV). Over time, by standing on God's Word instead of listening to my feelings, I gradually released the offense I'd been holding onto.

In the meantime, I realized that Satan's primary goal throughout our challenging season was to lead me to take offense toward God. If I hardened my heart toward God, Satan won the battle. By being angry with God instead of being angry with Satan, I was directing my anger and offense in the wrong direction.

At that time, I made a commitment to never again hold onto offense toward God for allowing trouble in my life. I had no way of knowing that my commitment would change the way I dealt with trials and challenges for the rest of my life.

Years later, as I processed the loss of my writing job, it would have been easy to blame God for closing the door on the opportunity. It also would have been easy to place blame or hold a grudge against the company. However, because I had spent years practicing the skill of remaining unoffended, the anger I felt after the job loss was short-lived. I worked through the anger, and, by the grace of God, I did not hold it against God—or against the company—when my writing dream fell apart.

Keeping a soft heart was essential for my healing.

When life hurts, it's tempting to hold onto offense toward God and others. Sadly, an offended heart quickly becomes a hard heart, and hard hearts always hinder the healing process.

If we are going to grow through life's rejections, we need tender and teachable hearts. Otherwise, our hearts won't be ready to receive the truth God wants to reveal as we grow.

As you process life's rejections, ask God to help you keep a malleable heart. Additionally, I challenge you to consider making the same commitment I made years ago. Will you commit to never again holding onto offense toward God when trouble comes? If you can make this commitment, the rejections of life will soon become foundations for tremendous growth. We'll explore this again in the discussion questions.

Now, let's shift our focus and examine the third way to grow through rejection: bringing shame into the light with others.

Light Dispels Shame

Earlier in this book, I encouraged you to ask God to show you an "inner circle" of trusted confidants who will point you to the truth and offer comfort in your weakest moments. When you bring stories of rejection and shame to your inner circle, these trusted friends can help you process your emotions and encourage you.

After losing my writing job, I didn't want to talk about it. However, I also knew that sharing my heart with my inner circle was an important part of accepting the situation and moving forward.

In the days and weeks following the painful phone call, I shared the difficult news with my closest loved ones. Processing the loss together helped me move toward a deeper level of mourning the loss. These friends and family members also offered space for me to verbally sort through my emotions.

I was surprised by the shift I experienced in my emotions as I shared the story with my family and close friends. Bringing the loss into the light dispelled the shame I was feeling. I sensed that shining the light on shame stripped its power. As I shared the burden of my heavy emotions with my loved ones, I felt free. I realized that the key to overcoming shame wasn't hiding; instead, I could move beyond the shame by sharing my feelings with others.

My loved ones also reminded me of God's truth and encouraged me. They looked into my eyes and said, "Stacey, you are not a failure. You are not lacking. You have nothing to be ashamed of."

I continued to process my emotions with my inner circle for months after losing the job. As we talked, they reminded me of God's character. They helped me recognize that God closed the door for reasons I couldn't understand, and they encouraged me to keep writing. I no longer felt like I needed to hide my disappointment from others. I was able to objectively talk about the facts of the situation and begin moving forward.

We all need these safe spaces where we can share life's rejections and disappointments. As paradoxical as it seems, bringing the shame attached to these difficult situations into the light strips away shame's power (1 John 1:5-7). Additionally, by sharing our losses with others, we create space for them to remind us that rejection does not define us. These loved ones can also encourage us by reminding us that God is trustworthy.

My loved ones regularly reminded me to keep trusting God with my writing. They also reminded me that God had a better plan. I had no idea of just how beautiful God's "Better Plan" would be.

Watching for God's "Better Plan"

Several months after I lost the writing job, my daughter Bekah approached me with an idea. She asked if we could write a mother-daughter devotional book together. Her vision was for mothers and daughters to read the book together and grow closer together while connecting with God in deeper ways.

I eagerly agreed, but in the back of my mind, I expected her to write one or two pages and lose interest. Instead, Bekah buckled down, and we wrote 60 devotions together.

As we wrote, I realized that I wouldn't have had the time to write a book with Bekah if I were still working with the large company. God closed the door with the company because he had a different plan for my writing career—a plan that far exceeded my greatest expectations.

Writing a book with my daughter was a once-in-a-lifetime opportunity. It was the greatest writing project of my life, and I wouldn't trade it for anything. We grew together, laughed together, and created a powerful resource to bless thousands of mothers and daughters. God's "Better Plan" for my writing career was far better than I ever could have imagined.

On a warm fall afternoon, Bekah and I received our first printed copy of our book. I realized that I would gladly trade a professional writing career with a prestigious company for writing one book with my daughter in a heartbeat. I also remembered the many moments when I told Jesus I trusted him—even though I didn't understand what he was doing. He had revealed his trustworthiness.

Multitudes of mothers and daughters are now using our book to strengthen their relationships and grow in faith together.

This story is a reminder that God's ways are not our ways, and his thoughts are not our thoughts. God's ways and thoughts are higher than ours (Isaiah 55:8-9). He is capable of redeeming life's most painful disappointments and rejections. You might not have hope that God can redeem your pain. I encourage you to draw close to Jesus and share your heart with him. Ask him to help you resist offense. Also, ask him to lead you to a trusted inner circle of people with whom to share your heart, and then begin watching for God's "Better Plan." God's plans for you are good, and he wants to fill you with hope.

Questions for Reflection and Discussion:

1. As you read this chapter, what painful rejection from your past (or present) came to mind? What step can you take today to move toward growth?

2. Describe a time in the past when a situation didn't make sense to you while it was happening, but God later used it for your good and his glory. How does reflecting on this situation give you hope for a part of your life that doesn't make sense to you right now?

3. Have you ever taken offense at God for allowing a troubling situation in your life? How did the spirit of offense affect your relationship with God?

4. Are you ready to make a commitment to never again hold onto offense toward God? What is holding you back from making this commitment?

5. Describe a time when bringing a shameful thought, incident, or situation into the light with another person dispelled the shame. If you've never had this experience, imagine how it might feel to share the story of a shameful rejection with someone you trust. This kind of vulnerability typically feels frightening at first; however, bringing shame into the light strips its power.

Epilogue

Before we conclude our time together, I invite you to join me in a place that's dear to my heart—our family's small cabin in the woods—and I'll leave you with a few final words about this journey into God's grace.

It's a cool summer morning, and I sit outside the cabin as songbirds awaken the dawn. It rained last night, and the forest smells like damp ferns and rich, black soil. I lean back in my chair as the sound of cartoons echoes from inside.

As I sip my coffee, I consider our plans for the day. I'm planning to head out for a long jog through the forested hills around the cabin this morning. Afterward, we'll take the kids to the hilltop in search of red-spotted newts, frogs, and turtles. By early afternoon, we'll return to the cabin for lunch, and I'll catch up on a freelance writing project while everyone watches TV and rests. Next, we'll head out on a hike, visit the reservoir to go fishing, and get ice cream before heading back to the cabin for a campfire. It will be a full day—a day filled with expectations and fun!

I'm thinking about everything I'll need to pack for each part of the day when I realize that what sounded fun in theory feels entirely overwhelming as we prepare to experience it. Cramming as much as possible into our weekend getaway feels grueling, not relaxing.

I'd like to pause to point out that 30-year-old Stacey would have ignored the sense of dread and pushed forward, determined to accomplish as much as possible. However, 42-year-old Stacey pays attention to the voice that says, *This is too much,* and pauses to talk to God about the day.

"Lord, I'm tired. Everything on our schedule for today feels exhausting. Show me what *you* want this day to look like," I pray.

I consider the journey I've been on—the journey of experiencing God's grace—and I sense that God is inviting our family to pursue life-giving rest instead of fitting as much as possible into the weekend.

Instead of lacing up my running shoes for a long run down the dirt road, I go inside the cabin, sit on the couch with my family, and make a suggestion.

"I know we had a full day planned today, but let's make sure we have time to rest and enjoy this trip. Let's talk about what we want to do today and make sure we're not cramming too much into this weekend," I offer.

The kids share ideas about what they'd definitely like to do, including catching cray fish, swimming, and eating ice cream. My husband wants to take a walk near his hunting spot on the hilltop. We adjust our plans accordingly, and by omitting a few activities—including fishing and hiking—we leave space for resting and playing.

The kids decide to start the day by building a fort with their dad behind the cabin, and they're gathering sticks for the roof when I set out for my morning run.

I'm just about to start jogging when something stops me. An unexpected thought comes to mind: *What if, instead of running, I took a slow morning stroll down this muddy road?*

The thought catches me off guard as I recognize that I don't *have* to run. I don't have to push my body harder than it wants to be pushed; I can apply the truth I've been learning and be gentle with my body. I can extend grace to myself today and begin at a slower, more restful pace. Perhaps beginning slowly will set the pace for the entire weekend.

As I stroll leisurely down the dirt road, I notice blackberries growing in the morning light, fragrant blossoms on a wild rose bush, and deer tracks on the sandy earth. A wood thrush sings on the hillside, and a solitary spring peeper cries out from a nearby beaver dam. I would have missed these gifts if I'd been running—moving too fast and breathing too hard to see and hear God's created world all around me.

I walk slowly for close to an hour and let the song of the wilderness wash over me. When I return to the cabin, I feel replenished and joyful. I haven't set any records for miles traveled or calories burned, but my heart is softer. I have just made one small step in the direction of the life I long to live—a life of peace and presence. God's grace has touched me.

Our family spends the rest of the day relaxing and making memories together. We build a morning campfire and let the woody smoke waft over us while we eat peanut butter and jelly sandwiches, bananas, and apples. My husband feeds the fire with moss-covered logs for hours, and we watch the wood turn to ash—intermittently stopping to play catch and add sticks to the kids' fort.

After an afternoon nap, we make time to catch cray fish, go swimming, and eat ice cream cones at Bob's Trading Post.

When the day draws to a slow close, I have not accomplished much in a measurable sense. However, I am more aware of God's presence with me. I am more aware of the precious gifts of my children and my husband. My pace has slowed. I feel rested and refreshed on a soul-level. As I sit by the flickering fire, I realize that I have encountered God's grace, and God's grace has changed me.

God is inviting you to experience this same grace, friend. He is inviting you to draw near to him in your weary, overwhelmed, broken-hearted, and fearful moments. He wants to work in your life to heal your heart, revive your soul, and lead you into his freedom.

Throughout our time together, we've done the hard work of facing our fears, naming our sins, identifying our insecurities, embracing our weaknesses, and more. We've learned how to create space for God to work in our lives by slowing down, being gentle with ourselves, extending grace to others, and bringing life's most painful emotions into the light.

From the bottom of my heart, thank you for taking this journey with me. Thank you for trusting me and sharing your time with me.

I pray that these pages have led you closer to the Father and helped you to grasp Jesus' love for you in deeper ways. As you continue to experience healing, redemption, and deliverance through God's grace, I pray that God's joy fills your life like never before.

Lastly, remember that God isn't asking you to be perfect. You will face setbacks as you grow in grace. You'll catch yourself eating chocolate in the pantry, snapping at your loved ones, or feeling paralyzed by fearful thoughts. Remember that leaning into grace is never a matter of trying harder or mustering up more willpower. Instead, God invites you to turn to him and let *him* accomplish what you cannot do for yourself. He's waiting with open arms. He wants to transform your life with his abundant grace.

Acknowledgments

As I reflect on the process of writing this book, I'm overwhelmed with gratitude for the support of many friends and loved ones. First, I thank my husband, Darrell, and our three children, Bekah, Caleb, and Aiden for supporting me, encouraging me, and standing with me through this process. You fill my life with joy and laughter, and I love you all.

Next, I'm deeply grateful for my dear friends and editors, Myra Balok and Beth Husband. Thank you for the months of work you have invested in this project. You have blessed me with the gifts of your precious time and energy, and you have shared invaluable feedback with love and thoughtfulness. You are both living representations of God's grace and love, and words cannot express my gratitude.

I am also deeply thankful for the friends who shared endorsements, prayed for me as I worked on this book, helped me launch the book into the world, and encouraged me not to give up. Thank you for believing in this project and carrying me through it with your prayers.

Mom and Dad, thanks for hanging out with the kids every week so that I could write. You are a gift to our family in so many ways. Thank you for always believing in my writing—even when

I was just a little girl filling notebooks with stories about beagle puppies.

Lastly, my heart overflows with gratitude for the God of all grace. Jesus, thank you for meeting me in my lowest moments, healing my heart, and leading me along this journey of grace. Your love and care have forever transformed my life. Thank you for pulling me from the darkness, working in my life, and filling me with your joy and peace. Every good gift in my life comes from you, and I give you all the glory.

Appendix A

99 Truths of Who You Are In Christ

These truths were compiled by Pastor Richard LaFountain. Check out Pastor Dick's powerful prayer resources at prayertoday.org

God says I am His . . .

1. Priceless Treasure - 1 Corinthians 6:20

2. Precious Jewel - Malachi 3:17

3. Priceless Vessel - 2 Timothy 2:20-21

4. Child - John 1:12

5. Masterpiece - Ephesians 2:10

6. Friend - James 2:23

7. Temple - 1 Corinthians 3:16

8. Co-laborer - 1 Corinthians 3:9

9. Soldier - 2 Timothy 2:3-4

10. Ambassador - 2 Corinthians 5:20

11. Building - 1 Corinthians 3:9

12. Cultivated Field - 1 Corinthians 3:9

13. Able Minister - 1 Timothy 4:6

14. Chosen - Ephesians 1:4

15. Beloved - Colossians 3:12

16. Inheritance - Deuteronomy 4:20

17. Witness - Acts 26:16

God says I am . . .

18. The Apple of His Eye - Deuteronomy 32:10

19. Complete in Him - Colossians 2:10

20. Sanctified Wholly - 1 Corinthians 6:11

21. Ready for the Master's Use - 2 Timothy 2:21

22. Loved Eternally - Jeremiah 31:3

23. Shielded by God - 1 Peter 1:5

24. Held in His Palm - Isaiah 49:46

25. Kept from Falling - Jude 1:24

26. Kept by the Power of God - 1 Peter 1:5

27. Not Condemned - Romans 8:1-2

28. One with the Lord - 1 Corinthians 6:17

29. Heaven Bound - John 14:1-2

30. Made Alive - Romans 8:11

31. Seated in Heavenly Places - Ephesians 2:6

32. Light in the Darkness - Ephesians 5:8

33. A Candle in the Dark - Matthew 5:15-16

34. A City on a Hill - Matthew 5:14

35. Salt of the Earth - Matthew 5:13

36. His Little Lamb - Psalms 100:3

37. A Citizen of Heaven - Philippians 3:20

38. Hidden with Christ - Colossians 3:3

39. Protected from Satan - 1 John 5:18

40. Secure in Christ - John 10:28-29

41. Set on a Rock - Psalms 40:2

42. A Super Conqueror - Romans 8:37

43. Born Again - 1 Peter 1:23

44. A Victor Not a Victim - 1 John 5:4

45. Healed by His Stripes - Isaiah 53:5

46. Covered by Jesus' Blood - Rev. 1:5

47. Sheltered under His Wing - Psalms 91:4

48. Hidden in the Secret Place - Psalm 91:1

49. The Head and Not the Tail – Deuteronomy 28:13

50. Strong When I Am Weak – 2 Corinthians 12:10

God says I have been . . .

51. Chosen before the World - Ephesians 1:4

52. Predestined to Be Like Jesus - Ephesians 1:11

53. Elected – Romans 8:29

54. Foreknown – Romans 8:29

55. Redeemed by the Blood - Revelation 5:9

56. Set Free from Sin's Bondage - Romans 6:18

57. Set Free from Satan's Control - Colossians 1:13

58. Set Free from Satan's Kingdom - Colossians 1:13

59. Forgiven of All My Trespasses - Colossians 2:13

60. Washed in the Blood - Revelation 1:5

61. Sealed by the Holy Spirit - 2 Corinthians 1:22

62. Adopted into God's Family - Romans 8:15

63. Justified Freely by Grace - Romans 3:24

64. Given a Sound Mind - 2 Timothy 1:7

65. Given the Holy Spirit - 2 Corinthians 1:22

66. Given All Things - 2 Peter 1:3

67. Given Great Promises - 2 Peter 1:4

68. Given the Ministry of Reconciliation - 2 Corinthians 5:18

69. Given Authority Over Satan - Luke 10:19

70. Given Access to God - Ephesians 3:12

71. Given Wisdom - Ephesians 1:7-8

God says I have . . .

72. All Things in Christ - 2 Peter 1:3

73. Living Hope - 1 Peter 1:3

74. Anchor to My Soul - Hebrews 6:19

75. Hope: Sure and Steadfast - Hebrews 6:19

76. Authority over Serpents - Luke 10:19

77. Power to Witness - Acts 1:8

78. Tongue of the Learned - Isaiah 50:4

79. Mind of Christ - 1 Corinthians 2:16

80. Boldness to Pray - Hebrews 10:19

81. Peace with God - Romans 5:1

82. His Faith - Luke 17:6

83. All Things for Life - 2 Peter 1:3

God says I can . . .

84. Do All Things Through Christ - Philippians 4:13

85. Find Mercy and Grace - Hebrews 4:16

86. Come Boldly to the Throne - Hebrews 4:16

87. Quench All the Fiery Darts - Ephesians 6:16

88. Tread on Serpents - Luke 10:19

89. Declare Freedom to Captives - Isaiah 61:1

90. Pray Always - Luke 21:36

91. Chase a Thousand Adversaries - Joshua 23:10

92. Overcome the Enemy - Revelation 12:11

93. Tread Satan under Foot - Romans 16:20

God says I cannot be . . .

94. Separated from His Love - Rom 8:35-39

95. Moved or Shaken - Psalms 16:8

96. Snatched from His Hand - John 10:29

97. Charged or Accused - Romans 8:33

98. Condemned - 1 Corinthians 11:32

99. Disappointed - Romans 10:11

Appendix B

How Does God See Me?

God rejoices over me.

"And as the groom rejoices over the bride,
So your God will rejoice over you" (Isaiah 62:5).

God wove me together in my mother's womb.

"For You created my innermost parts;
You wove me in my mother's womb" (Psalm 139:13).

I am wonderfully made.

"I will give thanks to You, because I am awesomely and
wonderfully made" (Psalm 139:14).

God delights in me.

"He will take great delight in you" (Zephaniah 3:17, NIV).

God sings over me.

"[God] will rejoice over you with singing" (Zephaniah 3:17,
NIV).

I am the apple of God's eye.

"Keep me as the apple of the eye" (Psalm 17:8).

I am God's beloved.

"My beloved is mine, and I am his" (Song of Solomon 2:16).

My Heart to Your Heart

Before we part ways, I invite you to join me as I sit beneath the poplar tree in our backyard on a warm summer afternoon. I feel inclined to share my heart and tell you about something that's deeply important to me.

Throughout our journey together in this book, you've come to know me well. You know that I tend to be driven and perfectionistic, and I've told you about my unhealthy habits and personal failures. Sharing these parts of my life feels vulnerable; nevertheless, I'm willing to share my story with the hope that my journey will help you find healing, restoration, and freedom, too.

As we conclude our time together, I feel led to give you a glimpse into one more part of my story: the season when I surrendered my life to Jesus.

I gave my life to Christ in the middle of a time when I was caught up in partying and making immoral decisions. I didn't know how to stop or change my behavior. However, I also knew that I wasn't living the life I desired. I turned to Jesus, asked him to help me, and committed to following him with my whole heart. Since that time, Christ has radically changed my life in wonderful and surprising ways.

Maybe you've been wrestling with the idea of surrendering your life to Jesus, too. Perhaps you've done unspeakable things, and you're sure Jesus won't accept you. You might be afraid that Jesus will ask you to walk away from something you're not ready to give up just yet.

Sadly, when we think we need to have our lives together *before* coming to Jesus, we have it backward. Jesus wants us to run to him in our messiness, brokenness, and sinfulness, and *he* will do the work of helping us honor him with our choices. This is a process, and it rarely happens overnight. It takes time, and the longer we seek Jesus, the more he works in our lives to help us become more like him.

Today, I gently invite you to consider where you are with Jesus. If you know that you've received Jesus as your Savior, then I pray that this book has helped you learn how to turn to him amid life's most challenging moments. I pray that you will continue to surrender every area of your life to him as you trust him to guide you. Conversely, if you've never surrendered your life to Christ and received his gift of salvation, then I encourage you to take this step today. Jesus has been pursuing you all of your life, and he is pursuing you at this very moment.

If you sense that Jesus is pursuing you and asking you to follow him, begin by humbly admitting that you need him. Tell him that you realize you have sinned and fallen short of God's perfect standards. Then, tell him that you believe that he died on the cross to take the punishment you deserve. Instead of punishing you through eternal separation, God loves you so much that he punished his precious Son in your place.

When Jesus died on the cross, he received the punishment you deserve. By believing that he took your place and receiving his free gift of salvation, you can be saved.

You can't do anything to earn this salvation. You only need to believe that Jesus died for you and receive him as your Savior. You can pray a prayer similar to this as a way of affirming your commitment: "Jesus, I believe that you died in my place, and I receive this gift. Thank you for forgiving my sins. I want to follow you. Come into my life and be my Lord and my Guide."

Jesus is pursuing you. Turn to him, and his love will transform your heart and your life.

As for me, Jesus has changed my life in remarkable ways. After surrendering to him, our relationship continued to strengthen and grow. His love empowered me to make slow changes over time. I now look back and hardly recognize the woman I once was.

The same can be true for you.

God's grace is waiting to meet you today. Will you lean into his grace?

Made in the USA
Middletown, DE
10 September 2024